GUIDING GIDEON

GUIDING GIDEON

Awakening to Life and Faith

Christopher Basil Brown

CASCADE *Books* • Eugene, Oregon

GUIDING GIDEON
Awakening to Life and Faith

Copyright © 2015 Christopher Basil Brown. All rights reserved. Except for brief quotations in critical publications or reviews, no part of this book may be reproduced in any manner without prior written permission from the publisher. Write: Permissions, Wipf and Stock Publishers, 199 W. 8th Ave., Suite 3, Eugene, OR 97401.

Cascade Books
An Imprint of Wipf and Stock Publishers
199 W. 8th Ave., Suite 3
Eugene, OR 97401

www.wipfandstock.com

ISBN 13: 978-1-62564-982-9

Cataloging-in-Publication data:

Brown, Christopher Basil

    Guiding Gideon : awakening to life and faith / Christopher Basil Brown.

    xviii + 148 p. ; 23 cm. —Includes bibliographical references.

    ISBN 13: 978-1-62564-982-9

    1. Spiritual direction—Christianity. 2. Storytelling—Religious aspects—Christianity. I. Title.

BV5053 .B75 2015

Manufactured in the U.S.A.

Scriptures taken from the New Revised Standard Version Bible. NRSV. Copyright 1989, by the Division of Christian Education of the National Council of the Churches of Christ in the U.S.A. Used by permission. All rights reserved.

Scriptures taken from The Message. MSG. Copyright © by Eugene H. Peterson, 1993, 1994, 1995. Used by permission of NavPress Publishing Group, All Rights Reserved. www.navpress.com.

Scriptures taken from the New King James Version. NKJV. Copyright © 1982 by Thomas Nelson, Inc. Used by permission. All rights reserved.

For Jim O'Connor and Allan Halladay:
two friends and guides in my journey of awakening to life and faith.

Contents

Preface: Imaging Creation ix
Acknowledgments xiii
Introduction: Taking the Deeper Pulse xv

Part I: Interior Life

1 Entering the Shadows 3
2 Following the Golden Thread 10
3 A Three-Sixty Turn 15
4 Separating Wheat from Chaff 20

Part II: Sacred Wounds

5 Light Shining in the Darkness 27
6 From Death to New Life 36
7 A Touch from Above 41
8 Full of Grace and Truth 47

Part III: Restoration

9 Initiation into New Life 53
10 On Earth as in Heaven 57
11 Recovering Lost Identity 61
12 In God Alone My Soul Finds Rest 65
13 Raised to Life 67
14 Establishing the Work of Our Hands 72
15 Defensive Batting 75

16 Beyond the Father Wound 78
17 Returning from Exile 81
18 It Is Written 85

Part IV: Experiencing Grace

19 Wild, Extravagant, and Unexpected Grace 89
20 Enlivening the Imagination 94
21 Wooed by Joy 98
22 Treasures in Jars of Clay 103

Part V: Participation

23 We Sat Down and Wept 107
24 A Road Less Traveled 111
25 Messengers from the Edge: Letters from Gideon 114
26 So Send I You! 121
27 From One Pilgrim to Another 124
28 Saying "Yes" to Love 128
29 Do You Love Me? 131
30 Embracing Servanthood 134
31 Wash All of Me 137
32 Can You Drink from This Cup? 139
33 Turning toward Jerusalem 142

Epilogue: Making Way for the New 145
Bibliography 147

Preface

Imaging Creation

As a spiritual guide, I have been fascinated by the way Michelangelo, the great artist and sculptor, was said to have imagined his *David* within a marble block and then worked to remove all that was redundant in order to bring his creation to near perfection. This incredible creativity leads me to ponder how the Creator of flesh and blood shapes human potentiality into the uniqueness and fullness of His imagination. Though the work of both sculptor and Creator in imagining human form remains a mystery, one works from the outside of the marble block inwards, whereas the other works from the inside outwards, breathing the image into the human heart to invite, nurture, and gently call it forth.

I wonder what it would have been like to be apprenticed to Michelangelo. Would I have started with fetching and carrying, erecting scaffolds, stoking fires, and sharpening tools? After practicing on castoff pieces of stone, would the master's request have come for me to chip away excess marble well away from the shape held in my master's mind? Would I ever have come close to that level of creative imagining, such incredible skill in bringing forth human shape from stone?

Though at my time of life there is little possibility of becoming a sculptor, I have been serving an apprenticeship in spiritual guiding and companioning. I began this apprenticeship as a pilgrim, with my director/guide encouraging me to be prayerfully attentive to my experiences and to the revelations of God's imagination for my formation, which often occurred in the midst of my life. Upon this foundation, I began to integrate more formal educative and fieldwork elements, slowly awakening to the Spirit calling me into an apprenticeship with the Creator in the care and guidance of souls. As I began to experience deeper resonance with gospel accounts of Jesus' *way* of guiding pilgrims—with his redeeming and transforming touch and his revelation of coming into the fullness of our humanity as we draw near the heart of God—I was filled with deep gratitude, awe, and reverence. For the art of companioning has brought me perilously close to the edge of mystery, a mystery that sharpens the distinctions between sculptor and Creator. For the former, human shape emerges from the marble as the stone yields to his will. Human growth into the fullness of the Creator's imaging is never a forced yielding, but rather a lifelong wooing of an often unrequited love.

I try to imagine Michelangelo at work in a cluttered and noisy workshop, with his apprentices laboring around him, attentive to his next command, knowing that whatever his idiosyncrasies or the fluctuations in his mood, creative genius was unfolding before their eyes. And yet, I wonder to what extent their master was able to reveal something of the heart and mind that held the image of his *David* in the years between 1501 and its completion in 1504. Michelangelo would have offered his apprentices glimpses of his *David* through models, drawings, and instructions, yet even so, they may have needed prompts and reminders.

At the height of accomplishment or the depths of despair, pilgrims often forget who they truly are and to whom they belong. This tragic loss of identity and communion stretches far beyond those few who seek out a spiritual guide or companion. It is endemic in societies and cultures that have forgotten that human fullness is an active and intentional quest. Too many of us settle into our existence as half-finished *Davids*, estranged from the image the Creator has left as a sacred deposit in our souls and numb to the prompts and wooing of love. Into this tragedy, spiritual guides and companions venture, but never alone. Whereas Michelangelo's senior apprentices may have had some tangible representations of what was in their master's mind, those charged with the care and guidance of souls are offered the revelation of the Creator's heart both in story (Scripture) and in person—Emmanuel, the God who, through the Spirit, is with us in the person of Christ.

If Michelangelo had come to the halfway point with *David*, only to discover flaws in the marble block, he might have had to abandon his work. But in the gracious and formative ways of the Creator, such flaws, imperfections, and fault lines don't halt the creative process. Rather, they provide entry points for the most profound movements of change, growth, and transformation.

PREFACE

When Michelangelo's *David* was unveiled in 1504, the magnificence of the human form was represented so near to perfection that it transfixed onlookers and transported them beyond themselves. To speak of the unveiling of the human pilgrim, we need to formulate a different language and a different way of perceiving as we awaken to the Creator's imagining placed as a sacred deposit within the pilgrim's soul.

The Creator's imagination woos us with gentle whispers and silence, with presence and absence, with encouragement and loving rebuke, ever calling us deeper into the life of the Trinity and a new heaven and a new earth. Jesus of Nazareth, the "true guide," models this way of living toward a new heaven and new earth through his human suffering, death, resurrection, and ascension, revealing how we might live as agents of reconciliation in the midst of our calamitous world, while also living out of the transcendent hope of an expansive imagination.

Guiding Gideon revolves around a series of guiding and companioning encounters with one of the Creator's young "Davids," a likeable young man of thirty-four named Gideon. We will journey alongside Gideon as he becomes more prayerfully attentive to the deeper rhythms of his experience and the sacred deposit of his Creator's imagination planted deep within his soul. His guide and spiritual companion, Julian Jacobson, is experienced in the care and guidance of souls, and he offers prayerful reflections following his encounters with Gideon in the companioning room. Julian is quick to acknowledge that he, too, is a pilgrim and experiences ongoing awakening along the way. Julian embraces both action and prayer, reminding us that guides need to bring encounters with pilgrims into the Creator's life-giving and formative imagination. Aware that coming into relationship with the Creator would awaken understanding and bring new meaning, Julian engages with ways of knowing and of coming to understanding that reflected an epistemology of love.

Gideon is a composite figure rather than one individual pilgrim. The construction of his identity has been influenced by the many pilgrims the author has companioned, without reference to any of their specific stories or personal details, for a spiritual guide receives the stories of individual pilgrims in strict confidence and sacred trust. Julian is an expression of the author and his experience as a social worker, an educator, a companion and guide of pilgrims, a spiritual director, and a pilgrim who has been guided and inspired by others. Julian's approach to guiding and reflecting is congruent with that of the author as it is presented in his previous book, *Reflected Love: Companioning in the Way of Jesus.*[1]

Before I bid you all welcome into Julian's companioning room, I want to acknowledge Michelangelo, who has assisted me in introducing some core themes. While Michelangelo was an artistic genius, he was also a pilgrim, and his creations on canvas and in stone, which were often lauded for their near perfection, emanated from the expansive imagination of his Creator, whether acknowledged or not, and from that sacred deposit placed within him.

Christopher Basil Brown
Ashgrove, Queensland, Australia
May 2014

---

1. Brown, *Reflected Love*.

Acknowledgments

I wish to express my gratitude to the many Gideons who have trusted me both as a guide and as a witness to the formative and transformative touches of the Spirit of God on their souls, and to my own spiritual guides who have held my soul journey in sacred trust.

I would especially like to thank Karen Hollenbeck Wuest, who as a gifted and committed editor has taken the essence of this work into her heart, and guided a rambling "pilgrim" manuscript onto the path of readability and clarity.

There are my friends, the holy scribblers—Irene Alexander, Jill Manton, Terry Gatfield, Neville Carr, John Steward, and Charles Ringma—who listened to roughly formed chapters and gave their ongoing encouragement and practical support. There are my long-term encouragers in this project, including Rob Jones, Penny Box, and Tania Cusack.

Finally, I wish to acknowledge my wife, Marilyn, who graciously and lovingly companioned me through the lengthy gestations of this work in its many forms.

Introduction
Taking the Deeper Pulse

Over the past two weeks, I have had two meetings with a young man of thirty-four, seemingly in the prime of his life, who sought me out as a guide. As some of the details of his life worked their way into conversations about his current distress, I gained the picture of a young man who had been gifted with a fine and creative intellect, who had already achieved considerable success in his profession of engineering, and who was held in high esteem by family, friends, and colleagues. Yet it was clear from his phone call to make a first appointment that all was not well.

When I met Gideon in our first session, I could tell by his faltering words, punctuated by long silences, that he was in turmoil, exhausted by the effort to hide his distress from those close to him. Though I could discern urgency within Gideon, I knew I had to exercise patience, for it was up to him to choose whether or not he would open the doorway into his darkened interior wide enough for both of us to enter.

Halfway through our second session Gideon recounted a reoccurring and distressing nightmare in which a fully developed young buck was being stalked by a pack of wolves. Previously, the surefooted buck had always outrun them, but last night, the buck had stumbled and been cornered by the pack. The dream had ended with the wolves baring their teeth and baying in triumph.

Close to the end of this session, Gideon relaxed for a moment. He had come to appreciate that his "inner wolves" had kept him running hard, especially through his work, which had preoccupied him over the last two years.

INTRODUCTION

After a long silence, he said, "You know, Julian, the edifice that I have built up around me is beginning to crumble, as if the foundations of the city tower block I've been building have concrete cancer."

When Gideon finally looked up and met my eyes, a glimmer of inner wisdom shone through his anguish. "Even as I speak of those concrete foundations, I wonder if there is something foundational I have neglected." Gideon paused. "There seems to be something locked away inside me." These words were followed by a deep sigh, and the session ended with more attention to his inner turmoil.

Even after hearing Gideon's words, I was concerned enough about the level of his distress to seek counsel from a consultant psychiatrist. This learned colleague voiced warnings about Gideon's depression, his reluctance to take antidepressants, and his past suicidal ideation. She listened graciously as I relayed Gideon's concern that the prescribed medication might mask his distress and stunt his desire to search for the "something locked away." I observed that I didn't feel Gideon's hold on life was tenuous, but rather that Gideon's complete absorption in work and his frantic efforts to amass great accomplishments were no longer sustaining him, leaving him with an unrelenting ache and feeling of emptiness and anguish. I wondered if darker and more desperate and destructive forces might need to emerge from the more hidden regions of his consciousness as part of his journey toward fuller restoration.

Knowing that this psychiatrist was sensitive to the spiritual dimensions of her patients' lives, I wondered if Gideon's reference to discovering "something locked away" might signal a yearning to transcend the confines of his self-centered desires and materialistic quests and come into relationship with something far greater.

"As you well know, Julian," the consultant psychiatrist reflected after listening to me, "there is much in our world to pull a young man down and into himself. There is also much of that interior world that remains a complete mystery to us. It doesn't sound like Gideon's looking for some fast track back to business as usual. If his agenda is deeper healing, growth, and what you have called 'fuller restoration,' then you're his man. He has sought you out as a guide and you've already begun taking his deeper pulse."

I remember sitting in my car outside the psychiatrist's office, somewhat amazed at how I had articulated, in her presence, those aspects of Gideon's story that I had almost bypassed. Her notion of taking Gideon's "deeper pulse" had struck a chord within me. Could Gideon's reference

INTRODUCTION

to his foundations and his acknowledgment of "something locked away" be invitations to greater and more abundant life? I certainly knew that to take Gideon's "deeper pulse," I would not be using sophisticated and objective diagnostic tools, but rather offering to accompany him through that slightly opened doorway into the midst of his anguish, fear, anxiety, and the torments of his mind, while reflecting to him the gentle and humble heart of the *One* I had come to call the "true guide." I knew that it would take courage to invite Gideon to journey into the darkness of his anguish, as such quests often draw us toward our deepest pain. I also knew that it would take faith to walk with Gideon through his anguish and beyond, trusting the Spirit to guide us toward the deeper foundations of his authentic selfhood, sacred identity, and purposeful vocation. I knew from the wisdom literature and from my own experience that these are to be found in the great mystery of our Creator-God, who is constantly forming, shaping, and restoring us. I wondered if part of Gideon's "depression" was in fact his being smitten by an existential and universal "homesickness," a hope deposited by the Creator-God in every soul as an invitation to move deeper into relationship with the Author of human life.[2]

As I returned to my office I knew that I needed to take time to prepare myself inwardly for my next meeting with Gideon, which was less than a week away. I was eager to discern the Creator's formative imagination for Gideon's restoration. However, on this occasion, my prayerful request for wisdom was met with silence. By entering into and remaining in this silence, the encouragement came to listen to the whispers of God's revelations from within Gideon's own experiences. This reminded me that the stepping stones for Gideon's restoration were not programs and methods for achieving fuller life, but rather openness to the prompts and guidance of the Spirit and greater unity with the person of Jesus as a true and trustworthy guide to the heart of the triune God.

As I continued my prayer, I asked the Spirit to enliven my intuitions and illuminate the eyes of my heart as I journeyed with Gideon. I acknowledged that this would require me to leave the relative safety of my diagnostic categories, theories, and methods so that both this young pilgrim and I, in the company of the Spirit, could step through the door of anguish and move into the hidden regions of the soul, where the deeper truth that Gideon sensed would be revealed. It was important for me to nurture faith in a transformative encounter between Gideon and the invisible presence

2. Eccl 3:11; Rom 6:23.

INTRODUCTION

of the Spirit. I hoped that Gideon would encounter belovedness where he had felt overwhelmingly alone, that he would discover abundance where he had experienced scarcity, and that he would experience healing and freedom where he had experienced wounding and bondage. To perceive the Creator's imaging of Gideon's fullest restoration, I would need to attune the ear of my heart to the whispers of God's revelation from within Gideon's story.

I trusted the community of the Trinity, who hold in their imagination the fully restored Gideon, to embrace us within their endless flow of self-giving, other-receiving, sacrificial love. Here, the buck of Gideon's dream can drink and there is a love stronger than the wolves seeking his destruction. In preparing to step through the doorway of Gideon's anguish and journey with him along a path of death and resurrection, I would need to drink this living water and press into this powerful and abundant love, for I, too, am being redeemed and restored to the fullness of the Creator's imagining.

The opportunity to continue to journey with Gideon came earlier than I had anticipated. A harrowing early morning experience caused him to seek a more immediate appointment, as if the wolves of his dream had moved even closer.

Part I:
Interior Life

1

Entering the Shadows

My invitation to Gideon at the beginning of our third session began with the question, "What is important for you to attend to this morning?" Gideon responded with a brief account of his troubled and restless night, which propelled him out of his apartment early and compelled him to visit his recently completed project and finest engineering achievement to date: the highly acclaimed, tall and imposing tower block quickly filling its commercial tenancies at the heart of the city. This enterprise had filled his waking moments for the past two years. Only a week before, Gideon had ridden the elevator to the highest observation deck, soon to become an expansive restaurant, to soak up the spectacular views with his boss who, with his left hand on Gideon's shoulder and with a great sweep of his right arm at the city below, had exclaimed, "With this project behind you at thirty-four, this world, my boy, is your oyster!" They had been gathering with other senior staff in the engineering firm to toast the coveted industry award that was now in Gideon's possession.

This morning, though, a dark cloud had eclipsed the sun, so that the glass and alloy façade of the building appeared dull to Gideon, rather than sparkling with light and glory, and the water droplets spraying from the fountain Gideon had strategically placed to the left of the main entrance seemed cold and dreary, rather than dazzling with light and life. These physical details matched the somber mood that had taken hold of him since he had toasted the project's success, and viewing the building no longer offered consolation to his troubled spirit or brought relief from the growing heaviness that had settled over his heart in the days and weeks following its completion.

In spite of the dread he felt as he entered the building, he had decided to ride the elevator so that he might bask in the expansive view of the city and remember his boss's proclamation. But in his haste to summon the lift, he had accidentally upset the cleaner's cart and found himself being chided for messing up *her* marble tiles. He timidly mumbled an apology to the angry cleaning woman and got on his knees to snatch up the scattered cleaning items, shocked that these carefully chosen and exquisite foyer tiles were no longer his. Hurrying away from the tower, Gideon did not stop to gaze at its impressive edifice, as he usually did. For the next hour, he stared at the coffee dregs and undissolved sugar in the bottom of his cup until a personified image of darkness reflected itself back at him, and he felt stirred to phone me. Gideon concluded this part of his account by expressing gratitude that I was available to see him this morning.

The pleading face of a schoolboy, who only hours before had looked up at the cleaner-cum-headmistress, was now fixed upon me. I breathed deeply and brought a gentle gaze into Gideon's rapidly oscillating eyes, wanting to reflect back to him my inner calmness and peace.

"You say that darkness reflected itself to you from the dregs of your coffee cup? What began to happen to you, Gideon, as you noticed that darkness?" I asked.

"This darkness moved up from the bottom of the cup to take hold of me and pull me down into the dregs," replied Gideon.

"To take hold of you and pull you down," I reflected.

"Yes," responded Gideon, "into a place where I am feeling sick of everything, overwhelmed and struggling to keep my head above water. This place is becoming very familiar—I seem to be stuck here."

I perceived these descriptions of Gideon's state as portals into his darkened "residence." Placing my full trust in this young man's innate knowing, I repeated the phrases back to him, counting them on the fingers of my left hand. "You say you're feeling sick of everything, overwhelmed and struggling just to keep your head above water. As we come to each of these, which one steps forward to invite your attention?"

Gideon chose "overwhelmed," and I stepped with him into the experience of that feeling.

I repeated the word *overwhelmed* and asked, "Gideon, what do you notice about overwhelmed?"

Gideon remained silent for a few moments. "I'm just so overwhelmed with everything," he said at last.

"You can experience being overwhelmed, but it is difficult to find words for what you are experiencing," I responded.

"Yes," he said.

"As you begin to talk about it, Gideon, do you notice yourself becoming overwhelmed?"

"I do. It's crept up on me as I've been sitting here, just like that darkness that pushed its way up from my coffee cup. Now it's starting to take hold of me."

"Can you slow that 'creeping up on you' down, as if you are observing it as it comes?"

Gideon lowered his head and closed his eyes.

I waited a few moments, then inquired, "As you carefully observe 'overwhelmed' coming, what do you notice happening?"

"This is very strange," Gideon replied. "As I observe 'overwhelmed' coming, it's turning into a roadway, and I can see myself walking down this asphalt road."

Calmly and gently, I responded, "As you observe 'overwhelmed' coming, you notice the figure of yourself walking down an asphalt road." In repeating back what Gideon had disclosed, I validated his unfamiliar experiences and invited him to continue his observation.

Gideon closed his eyes, dropped his head and remained silent. Without looking up he began to speak.

"As I observe the figure of myself walking down this asphalt road it seems that all the past events, my worries and concerns, and those dark and distressing thoughts, those endless negative commentaries, and those dark crippling emotions, which have been relentlessly bombarding me for weeks, even months, have begun to assemble along one side of that roadway. In fact, they are evenly spaced along that roadside." Gideon paused and looked up.

"As you witness all these entities that have been bombarding you assemble on the side of the roadway, what do you notice beginning to happen to you?"

"I am noticing something very strange. In my darkest times they all come at me at once, just like the wolves in my dream closing in on that buck. Now that they are evenly spaced, I am wondering if it would be possible to tackle them one by one. But even as I say that, there is a voice urging against this, and the fear that was always present in the middle of that bombardment is back with me again."

Noticing the distress on Gideon's face I gave a summary of what he had said, then asked, "Can you say something more about the voice and the fear?"

"They are so annoyingly familiar," Gideon replied with irritation. "They're just like those wolves stalking the buck, following me here to your room, and creeping up behind me on the asphalt road. Even as I say that, I can feel my anger rising."

"Can you slow that down a little, Gideon, just as if you were now observing your anger rising?"

"Yes, I can," he replied, his voice calmer. "Up until this moment, I would become so angry with what I am calling the wolves that my anger would quickly get out of control and then join them. Now, as I observe it rising, it hesitates, as though checking to see if I need it on my side."

Gideon's voice dropped. While his next words were barely audible, I am sure he was inviting anger to stay on his side. "This is going to sound very strange, but I am getting used to strange things happening in your room! When anger knew he was needed, he invited courage to join us, and the resolve that is building within me is to continue down the asphalt road, despite the voice cautioning me that I will lose everything I have worked so hard to achieve."

"And what do you choose to do?" I asked.

"I choose to continue down the road," Gideon responded.

During the next ten minutes I inwardly wondered if Gideon's resolve would hold and his courage remain. The life Gideon witnessed emerging in front of him as he continued down the road appeared drab and lifeless, in black and white, with the people well known to him appearing as cardboard cutouts. As he passed by these representations, these friends and counselors urged him back to his "normal" reality, even mimicking the voice that had insisted he had too much to lose. When Gideon encountered the cutout figure of the doctor who had recently diagnosed depression and prescribed pills, his image faded before he had even written his prescription. Then Gideon reported that the asphalt road had begun to peter out into what he described as "a no man's land."

At this juncture Gideon saw his parents, and though he would have loved to stop and embrace them, he said there was a strong residue of ambivalence, anger, and bitterness standing in the way. Just beyond his parents, the road became dark, and Gideon hesitated on the edge of this darkness. In the silence that followed, Gideon became more and more distressed.

I asked, "Gideon, as you witness yourself hesitating on the edge of this darkness, what do you notice is beginning to happen inside?"

"This overwhelming grief is rising up inside me. I'm wondering if what that voice was saying about losing everything was true. For images of all I've been working for over the past few years—the projects, the awards, the people who have praised my achievements—have been swallowed up in that darkness, leaving me totally gutted and empty. Even as I say that, I can glimpse my office—a place of commitment, creativity, drive, and energy—and it looks so desolate."

Gideon doubled up, his hands covering his face and his elbows resting on his knees.

"At this very moment," he whispered, "I feel as if the wolves have finally got their buck!"

After a few moments of silence, Gideon raised his head so that his eyes appeared just above his fingertips.

With my eyes on his, I reflected back the words he had spoken.

"What you have experienced at the edge of the darkness has left you feeling gutted and empty, wondering if the wolves have finally got their buck."

"Yes!"

"As you stay with that gutted and empty grief, can you see what your attention is being drawn to next?"

A long pause followed before Gideon spoke again.

"Though all is dark, I think I glimpse a path ahead."

"As you notice the path in that darkness, what do you choose to do?"

"I choose to continue on it," Gideon replied.

As Gideon inwardly continued down the pathway, I felt a surge of courage rise within my chest. After several minutes, Gideon reported that in front of him on the roadway was the looming personification of darkness, engulfing the eerie landscape in black and grey. Gideon began to shiver and said he felt cold and scared. As I noticed my own shivering, I reminded myself that, with the Spirit alongside us, there could be light amidst the overwhelming darkness.

As Gideon's inner eyes became more accustomed to the darkness, he noticed that this entity was made up of many parts, and he could make out a host of dark and sinister figures lurking behind the trees and beneath the bushes in this strange and shadowy territory. Gideon likened them to the wolves stalking the buck, getting ready to pounce and tear him to shreds. He froze in the middle of the path, ready to flee, go back the way he had come.

"What would it be like to eyeball these dark and sinister figures?" I asked gently, so that my question would not place him under additional pressure.

"It's a struggle to open my eyes, as if I am that cornered buck. I wish I had a full set of antlers to protect myself. Even though I have anger and courage, I still feel dread, as if the wolves are closing in for the kill."

"These shapes are familiar, but as you encounter them now, they seem to be closing in and they fill you with dread."

"Yes," Gideon replied. "I have been trying to look at them out of the corner of my eye, but I'm afraid of how they might respond."

"As you look at them out of the corner of your eye, what do you notice you need to do next?"

"I need to eyeball them more directly," Gideon replied, "but I have to put on courage and anger as I might put on the deer's antlers."

"Are you able to do that?"

"Yes," he said, "I believe I can do it."

Tentatively, Gideon began to eyeball each figure along the pathway. As he took full measure of each shape and entity, his progress along the path slowed.

"There are all these shapes clamoring for my attention like figures in a crowd all wanting to be heard at once." He paused, then added, "It is almost as if they want to talk to me."

"What would it be like to listen to them?" I asked.

"I want to listen, but when I look in their eyes, I feel my old fear that anger will desert me and join the wolves. I see rage in their eyes!"

"If you continue to observe the fear and rage in their eyes, what do you notice?" I asked.

Gideon waited, and I saw that he was more relaxed. When our eyes met, he looked sheepish.

"I'm really ashamed to admit to this, Julian, but the eyes of these shapes are mirroring back to me what I have been feeling inside. It's not them—it's me! I'm keen to engage them, but I'm not sure where to begin."

"What is it that you would most like to learn from them?" I inquired.

"What they are doing in my life," Gideon replied.

"You might just engage them one by one and ask, 'What is it that you are doing in my life?'"

After a few minutes, Gideon said, "They are using words like 'help,' 'protect,' 'keep alert,' 'warning.' Up till now, I have felt totally bombarded by them all pounding on my door day and night. Now I am feeling like a neglectful parent who has locked out the teenagers because they were untidy and their music was loud. When I answered the door, I discovered the 'teenagers' all had names and seemed to be more for me than against me."

In the period of silence that followed, I imagined Gideon sitting on the pavement, surrounded by oddly dressed teenagers.

Then Gideon said, "Some have come close, but others seem shy and are holding back. Some are hardly even visible from the path, but I can hear their faint cries of distress in the background. As I say that, the feeling of overwhelmed has returned. You know, I think they're trapped or imprisoned!"

"You are noticing the feeling of overwhelmed and you think some of these shyer 'teenagers' are distressed, trapped, or imprisoned," I said.

In the silence that followed, I sought to be attentive to Gideon's demeanor and my own intuition. His countenance had softened into humility and gentleness, and all residues of apprehension, cynicism, and suspicion had vanished. With tears on his cheeks, Gideon announced that a new friend, "grief," had offered to accompany him as he moved further down the path.

"'Grief' and 'courage' seem to know each other, along with that part of anger that is on my side."

In the safe company of "grief," this session found its haven of rest, and Gideon and I scheduled time for a meeting the following week.

2

Following the Golden Thread

On the evening of my third session with Gideon, I spent time prayerfully reflecting on the richness of our encounter and upon those aspects of Gideon's story and experiences that resonated deeply with my own. Whenever I am confronted with distress and emotional turmoil in a pilgrim's life and with the mysterious rhythms and flows of her inner stories, imagery, and parables, I seek the quiet of prayerful solitude, where I can hold both the pilgrim and myself within the tender and compassionate gaze of tranquility and contemplation. Sinking beneath the worry-filled noise of ordinary, everyday awareness, I find calm waters as I rest in the love of the One who stilled the storms.

Something of a role reversal occurs in this place of rest and receptivity. In the morning's session I embodied and reflected the calm receptiveness of the stiller of storms in order for Gideon to enter and attend to his stormlike experiences; now, in the restful presence of my true guide, I become the pilgrim. By inviting the Spirit to guide me through my own inner responses and reactions—my inner resonance—to Gideon's experiences, I discovered the gift of his story for my ongoing journey of life and faith and for my growth and development as a guide.

The Spirit was not slow to respond to my invitation. An invisible hand reached in through the doorway of my active and believing imagination to place before me a ball of multicolored wool. With this colorful image came the memory of these lines from a William Blake poem:

> I give you the end of a golden string,
> Only wind it into a ball:
> It will lead you in at Heaven's gate,
> Built in Jerusalem's wall.[1]

I realized that the image and poem had been offered as trustworthy guides for my prayerful reflection as I re-entered my morning's encounter with Gideon. If we had both walked through a dark storm, then here was a lifeline, the end of which I was to hold. As I did so the ball of wool rolled through a doorway, which I recognized as the entrance into Gideon's darkness, the same doorway that had swung slightly ajar in our first two meetings and then today had opened just wide enough for us both to squeeze through. Gideon, however, had been dramatically drawn into that doorway by the unsettling picture of darkness moving up from the bottom of his coffee cup to pull him down into the dregs.

Though I had been only slightly hesitant to enter into that darkness during the morning's session, I now balked as I revisited that same entrance. I tried to convince myself that I had lost much of my fear of the dark by awakening to its presence within me, and by guiding pilgrims through what the psalmist calls "the valley of the shadow of death,"[2] but there was enough residue of fear to cause me to pause and to take notice.

Then a tiny thread of gold woven through the length of the wool caught my eye. For a fleeting moment, it seemed to catch fire and run through the wool like a lit fuse, burning brightly but not consuming the strands twisted around it. The Spirit, the "Living Flame of Love,"[3] had squeezed in through that doorway with Gideon and me. In the presence of the One who stilled storms, the residue of fear that had caused me to falter at the doorway of Gideon's darkness delivered me to the doorway of my own poverty of spirit, the doorway of the true guide's first Beatitude: "Blessed are the poor in spirit, for theirs is the kingdom of heaven."[4] Naming this doorway "poverty of spirit" was a real awakening. The action of stepping in solidarity with Gideon through this entrance into the unknown, and then being drawn back to attend to it in my prayer and reflection, opened a window into the first Beatitude, where I entered the true guide's journey of life and faith and was embraced in the true guide's love. The golden thread that leads us in at

---

1. Blake, "Jerusalem," VI, lines 1–4, in *Poems of William Blake*, 250.
2. Ps 23:4 KJV.
3. John of the Cross, "Living Flame of Love," 22.
4. Matt 5:3 NRSV.

Heaven's gate enables us to transcend our normal reality so that we might live our lives out of the alternative imagination of the kingdom of Heaven.

Then my mind lighted upon Gideon's mysterious account of being accompanied by the entity of "grief." If Gideon's doorway was darkness and my doorway was "poverty of spirit," then "grief" was the "mourning" of the second Beatitude, with its promise of divine comfort—a comfort that destabilizes us in order to console us.[5] In following the true guide's journey of life and faith, Gideon was drawn into a spacious place where he could grieve the loss he faced when much of his identity—his projects, accomplishments, supporters, and status—was swallowed up by that dark void.

I was infused with hope that by stripping away all that estranges us from our self, from others, from our created world, and from God, we would be drawn nearer to the meekness and humility of the true guide's third Beatitude: "Blessed are the meek, for they will inherit the earth."[6] In following the golden thread of the "Living Flame of Love," I knew that both Gideon and I would awaken to our true identity, vocation, and inheritance in God alone. This reminder of the true guide's way helped me attend to the stopping place of the rolling ball of wool at Gideon's grief, as if the wolves of his dream had finally got their buck. As a guide, I cannot expect immunity from the grief that rises up when all that has sustained us is lost. Perhaps the ball had stopped here to encourage me to watch and pray rather than hurry through Gideon's story. As I attended to Gideon's powerful metaphor of the wolves and the buck, I felt Gideon's fear and my own growing sense of powerlessness.

As I waited, watched, and prayed in this dark, tomblike place, two images emerged. First, I saw a young man gazing up at the imposing and shining edifice of a city tower, clutching a trophy close to his chest, saying, "All of my creation" over and over again. Second, I saw the same young man, weeping amidst the ruins of his imploded tower. Yet as I observed him, he shrank to the size of a child surrounded by a pile of Legos. As I connected with this child, I experienced a strong feeling of abandonment, for the child surrounded by Legos was completely alone. Then the child grew into Gideon, who had placed all his energy into building around himself an edifice of steel, concrete, and glass, relegating the child's experience of aloneness to a tiny locked room.

---

5. Matt 5:4.
6. Matt 5:5 NRSV.

Such images could easily be blinked away as daydreams, yet, as I acknowledged them as a prompting of the Spirit, I experienced a profound solidarity between Gideon as pilgrim, me as flesh-and-blood guide, and the true guide as present through the Spirit. God, who is present in the midst of our lives, had lifted the veil just enough to reveal His Father-heart for Gideon. With this glimpse, I had faith that the wounds that had established restricted trajectories in Gideon's life could be transformed into sacred doorways into the Holy. As his guide, I just had to be willing to follow the golden thread.

In one of our earlier sessions, Gideon had suspected that there was something locked away within. Could this be the lost child, or was there more? Again, I glimpsed the ball of wool and moved on, trusting the golden thread to guide me even further into the truth that Gideon was finding the courage to follow, even if it meant walking down a pathway to confront the dark and sinister figures who had personified darkness to him.

As Gideon eyeballed the figures, my attention was focused on the wool. Despite the darkness, I could detect that tiny thread of gold that had previously spoken to me of the accompaniment of the Spirit. The ball of wool left the pathway and encircled three figures in ancient dress, who presented themselves as Noah, Abraham, and Moses, each of whom had ventured out with a slender thread of faith to follow the way of their God, often at great cost to themselves. It was as if the solidarity I had experienced with Gideon and Jesus just moments before was extending to include others of faith.

This thread of faith had led Noah to place his trust in things not yet seen and to build an ark to save his family. Abraham had followed this thread away from his own land and security to venture into what was unknown, even to become a stranger and alien. Moses had followed this thread of faith when he had chosen not to be known as a son of Pharaoh's daughter, but rather to be mistreated along with the oppressed people of God. In keeping faith with this deeper truth, he confronted the might of the Egyptian empire and led his people out of their captivity—but also away from their place of security, into a desert.

As these three characters entered the context of my guiding Gideon, three pressing questions began to surface. Was I being asked to place my trust in things unseen? Was I prepared to leave the security of companioning theories and methods to venture with Gideon into the unknown? What captivity might I need to be led out from in order to walk in greater freedom with Gideon? But as these questions arose, the cloud of witnesses encircled by the wool grew in number, all of whom had left safety and security to journey on this lesser-known pathway.[7] I saw the disciples of Jesus, who had left their nets and livelihoods to move along the uncertain pathway of their prophetic guide, and they seemed to be inviting me to join them in this great journey of faith, hope, and love. Then I saw Jesus, his face set in the direction of Jerusalem, knowing that his solidarity with broken and suffering humanity would bring him humiliation, betrayal, suffering, and death.

Then the cloud of witnesses departed, and I gathered up the length of wool that had encircled them. The slender and barely visible golden thread woven through the wool had guided me through my time of prayer and reflection, inviting me to trust in things unseen. If I was to leave what had been secure I was not alone, for the true guide would lead me out of captivity and offer me his freedom. This was hope! In the august company of the disciples and veterans of faith, all of whom had let go of what they might have been to set out to quench their deep and compelling thirst for union with God, I was invited to journey with Gideon, trusting the way to unfurl—like the ball of wool—before us.[8]

As my time of prayer and reflection came to an end, I set aside the ball of wool and caught a glimpse of Gideon walking down the darkened pathway in the company of his new friend, "grief." He reminded me of the disciples who had left their nets and livelihoods to follow Jesus into the unknown, and I was keener than ever to take that journey with him. It was this glimpse of a determined Gideon, along with the love, faith, and hope that had been re-enlivened in me during this time of prayer and reflection, that prepared me for our next meeting.

---

7. Heb 11.
8. Heb 12:1–2.

3

A Three-Sixty Turn

At the beginning of our fourth session, I asked Gideon what he needed to attend to, and he returned to the moment when he had been walking down a darkened pathway in the company of the emotions that had previously overwhelmed him. As Gideon turned down this darkened pathway, another sinister and threatening figure moved out from behind a tree to block his way. He paused and looked at me.

"As that dark and sinister figure moves out from behind the tree to block your way, what do you notice happening to you?"

"I can feel that fear rising up within me," Gideon responded as he drew back in his chair.

"What are you noticing?"

"The figure is puffing itself up to look bigger. And as it does that, I see myself shrinking."

"As it puffs up to look bigger, you are noticing yourself shrink," I reflected.

"Not only am I shrinking, but I'm feeling rather naked. Julian, do you remember our last session, when my projects, achievements, awards, and supporters were all swallowed up in that dark void? It seems as if part of me has been swallowed with them, and I have lost my protective armor. I'm so small in the face of this overbearing figure who seems to be gloating over my losses and my inability to respond."

Gideon dropped his head and placed his hand on his forehead. "I don't know what to do," he continued. "And as I say that, I have a picture of me turning around to go back and reclaim my protective armor. You know,

Julian," he added, looking toward me, "I thought I had progressed further than this. Now I'm slipping backwards!"

I paused, then reflected back what Gideon had said. "As you see the figure of yourself turn away, what do you notice happening within and around you?"

Gideon remained silent, then began to describe the scene unfolding before him.

"As I look at the small, unprotected image of myself, I see raw emotions instead of my work projects and achievements. But as I observe grief, loss, anger, aloneness, anxiety about the future, and shame at my thought of turning back, some of the emotions are taking on shapes and colors of their own. 'Grief' is the most prominent, and 'courage' is standing in the background, but they are all gathering around me, exhorting me to turn around and face the sinister figure."

"What do you choose to do?" I asked.

"I can feel a real tension." Gideon grimaced. "The pull to turn back has become even stronger. I know that all was not well in my former life, and I can acknowledge that my absorption in work had a driven, addictive edge to it. The more I fed it, the more it demanded. Though I would have been very angry if someone had said, 'Gideon, do you realize you are becoming a workaholic?' But even the thought of going back to all of that—of doing more and more of what sustains me less and less—makes me shudder and fills me with dread. Now the figure of me is running furiously, and he's just collapsed in a heap."

"Can you stay for a moment with that running figure of you who has just collapsed?"

"I'm aware that I have actually been running from something important to me, something locked within, like that inner truth we spoke about in our early sessions. Running has brought me to this place of collapse."

"As you say that, Gideon, what happens to the collapsed figure?"

"He's in a quandary—between the life he knows, which will no longer sustain him, and the unknown. But I can't solve his problem, even though I have made a career out of being a problem-solver."

"The figure of you is in a quandary between the life you know, which no longer sustains you, and that which is unknown. This has brought you to a place of collapse, because you have been running away from something deep within you. And the unknown is not a problem that you can use your skills to solve."

A THREE-SIXTY TURN

"As I hear you say it, I see it is more about a choice. The unknown in front of me involves a leap of faith."

In the expectant silence of the moments that followed, I felt an inner shift as I dwelt on Gideon's expression: "leap of faith." I had a fleeting image of the disciples leaving their nets to follow Jesus.

"It's a real leap," said Gideon, breaking the silence. "It's like those disciples leaving everything to follow Jesus. And now I know I have to face up to what is blocking my path!"

Gideon took a deep breath. "I have turned around to face the enemy, which looks like a dragon. When I try to catch its eyes, it looks away and snorts fire and smoke in my direction. In some ways it amuses me, for it's like a dragon trying to inflate its ego. But there is a sinister edge that I have to take seriously."

"You are discerning that there is a sinister edge," I reflected.

"I wish I could name it! You know when Jesus asked the unclean spirit in the wild man who lived among the tombs, 'What is your name,' and the reply was, 'My name is legion, for we are many'? It seems just like that. The dragon is made up of many parts."

"What happens as you notice that the dragon is made up of many parts?"

"Those emotions that encouraged me to eyeball the dragon are whispering that the dragon's real name is 'fear.' I am also noticing that 'anger' has begun to relax. My emotions have begun to settle, my mind is clearer, and my heart is more in tune with what is happening. I feel wide awake!"

"As you feel wide awake, what do you notice about the dragon?"

"The dragon is fear, but his scales are made up of all my different fears, and as I look closer, I see they all have names: my fear of the unknown, my fear of losing favor with my supporters, my fear of losing my status and esteem . . ."

Gideon faltered and wiped his eyes. "The dragon is shrinking, but still blowing smoke, as if to hide from me what I am really afraid of."

"Can you get a sense of what it is you are really afraid of?" I asked gently.

Gideon's next words were barely audible, but it sounded like a conversation with "grief." When he looked up there were tears rolling down his cheeks.

"The dragon is very small and I can glimpse a tear in its eye. I had a stuffed toy dragon just like it when I was a child. I remember hoping it would protect me from danger—and this seems to be what the dragon in front of me has been trying to do with all its ridiculous puffing. There is a lot of grief and pain down here," Gideon said, pointing toward his gut. "There is something locked away that the dragon of my fear has been guarding for many years, convinced that something in me will die if I go there. What a sorry sight we are now, feeling sorry for each other."

I waited before interrupting what was transpiring between this weeping pair. "Gideon, you mentioned a 'sinister edge.' Does that edge still need your attention?"

"There was a dark shape that piggybacked on all my fears, as if to glue them together and use them against me."

"Use them against you," I repeated.

"That 'evil edge' conspired to keep me captive, to keep me running, to keep me away from real life. The edge is my addictiveness and workaholism, my insatiable appetite for more and more of what sustains me less and less—what has brought me a whisker's breadth from destruction."

Gideon clenched his fists and beat them on his knees. His tear-stained face reddened, and I wondered if "anger" had risen up again. "So destructive! So destructive!"

After a silence pregnant with regret and pain, I felt my own regret over how easy it had been for me to become preoccupied with projects and success, so that I hardly noticed how estranged I had become from the depth of my own soul, from significant others, from the created world around me, and from my God. To come face to face with this destruction, as I had some years ago, was painful even in its remembrance. As Gideon repeated the words "so destructive," I inwardly repeated the prayer, "Lord have mercy on me; Lord have mercy on me," which guided my focus back to Gideon, who had begun to relax.

"Now that I have named my real enemy, I wonder if I might separate from the dragon of my fears." Gideon paused and placed a hand on his heart. There was a smile on his tear-stained face. "Why, I feel a flicker of compassion, and the dragon seems more of a friend! It's no longer blocking my path."

"Separate from the dragon of your fears," I repeated, "who seems more of a friend."

"If the 'evil edge' could be separated, then perhaps my dragon might shift from 'fear' and accompany me with 'grief' and the others along this pathway."

"Gideon, you have acknowledged the need for the evil edge to be separated. Could you stay with that for a minute?"

"I am beginning to feel that I need to make something of a confession." After a weighty silence, he began, in a voice tinged with regret. "You know, Julian, I have to acknowledge not only the cost of this destructive energy to me and others, but also how I have colluded with it. I was the one who fed it. I was the one who did all I could to ignore those inner niggles that I was not keeping faith with a deeper truth. I was the one who became so self-preoccupied that I shut out those close to me. Even in my attendance at church, and those times when I would run out of excuses not to attend my Bible study group, I was deliberately distancing myself from those in my community of faith. And even as I think of it now, I craved the affirmation and admiration of my boss and colleagues more than the words of God for my life."

Gideon had begun to weep, and I felt the stirring of the Spirit. In this holy moment I could discern the deep sorrow and repentance that flowed beneath his words of confession.

After some moments Gideon continued:

"And before you, Julian, and before my God, I wish to express my deep sorrow and regret for my sinfulness, and my desire that I be separated from the influence of such an 'evil edge,' and I ask for the forgiveness of Jesus."

"So Gideon," I responded, "you have confessed your sins, indicated your sorrow and regret and your desire to separate from the influence of evil, and you have asked for the forgiveness of Jesus."

"Yes!"

"Then in the name of Jesus, I offer you his forgiveness. Thanks be to God for His love and mercy and for the redemption offered through Jesus, His son."

"Thanks be to God," responded Gideon.

4

Separating Wheat from Chaff

There are moments in my reflective and prayerful solitude where I find myself rapt in awe, as if the world around me is filled with the grandeur of God, waiting for my spiritual sensibilities to awaken. On the evening following my morning's session with Gideon, I sat with the mystery of how Gideon's confession had emerged. I was not seeking a logical and linear explanation, for I knew I couldn't pry into mystery. In my prayer, the wings of my mind had gently folded, enabling my conscious awareness to glide down into the more spacious and integrated place of my heart. My wonderment and reverence intensified at the glimpse I had been given of a flicker of God's Spirit lighting upon human experience and of being privy to the illuminated soulscape of another mortal being.

How could Gideon's almost debilitating fears be connected together and reworked into the shape of a dragon—a dragon blocking his pathway? How could this dragon shape be portrayed on his inner visual screen in a way that he could actively engage with it? I am always in awe at the deep mystery of our God-given faculty for active and believing imagination. What a privilege to witness this dramatic, implausible encounter, which had led Gideon to significant and life-giving insights! I was invited to observe Gideon's inner parable as it vividly played out before him, bringing him face-to-face with the destructive and life-eroding parts of himself. This "parable" invoked his deeper spiritual awareness, enlightening the eyes of his heart.[1]

---

1. Eph 1:18.

In the sacred place of my reflection, I could see that in ordinary everyday awareness, Gideon could easily have reframed his inner turmoil as "depression" caused by a chemical imbalance, an imbalance that could occur in the life of such a creative high achiever who comes to the end of one of his biggest projects. But thanks be to God that this graphic and powerful representation of what was most real in Gideon's life had brought him to a place of heart-felt repentance, a *metanoia*, a three-hundred-and-sixty-degree turn on the firm and trustworthy axis of his true guide, the *One* who is light and life for both Gideon and for me. As I was drawn back to this turning, tears welled-up in my eyes and my heart pounded!

Entering as guide and pilgrim through the doorway of our poverty of spirit and embarking on this faith-life quest, Gideon and I both needed to turn around, wake up, and enter dimensions of our lives beyond the scope of our ordinary, everyday awareness. We needed to turn our gaze inwards and come face-to-face with the hidden dimensions of our lives that had totally overwhelmed us. In this movement of *metanoia*, Gideon had unmasked fear, a persuasive and somewhat sinister force safeguarding him from his own reality. This sentry had, for much of his life, stood guard at the threshold of his inner landscape, protecting him from the painful truth of his own history. While as his guide, I had endeavored to keep him attentive to what was emerging directly in front of him, now in the privacy of my prayer and reflection, I had the opportunity to be attentive to my resonance with Gideon's experience and face the residue of sinister forces keeping me from my own reality.

My reflection drew me to two disparate elements of Gideon's account. First, the incident he had described in an earlier session, when his boss had put an arm on his shoulder at the celebration for his industry award and, with a sweep of his arm at the city below, had exclaimed: "With this project behind you at thirty-four, this world, my boy, is your oyster!" Second, I was drawn to his reference to the "sinister edge" that had piggybacked on all his fears, as if to glue them together and use them against him. In holding together these two elements of high praise and the "sinister edge," I witnessed a third image joining them: the gospel account of Jesus being taken by the devil to a very high mountain to be shown all the kingdoms of the world and their splendor. "All this I will give you . . . if you will bow down and worship me."[2]

---

2. Matt 4:8–9.

Though I had missed this connection until that moment, I wondered where it was taking me in my own story. Was there a dragon being piggybacked by a "sinister edge" in my path? Then I heard the voice of the psychiatrist I had consulted about the nature of Gideon's distress saying, "If his agenda is deeper healing, growth, and what you have called 'fuller restoration,' then you're his man. He has sought you out as a guide and you've already begun taking his deeper pulse." The dragon must have puffed-up its ego, because my own pulse quickened and indignation seeped into my veins.

What masks our vision and prevents us from eye-balling the dragons which stand in the path of our fuller embrace of the light and life of the true guide? I did not doubt that both Gideon's boss and the consultant psychiatrist were good people. But could I discern the subtle dark shapes that co-opted their words and twisted their intentions to entangle our motives and deepen our enculturation in the success and status orientations of our dominant societal imagination? Was my desire to guide pilgrims in the *way* of Jesus, while also seeking the acclaim and affirmation of my colleagues as a guide-companion? My indignation and resistance settled, and my awe and wonder returned for how Gideon's interior life had been presented to him in visual and parabolic forms. During those pregnant moments, the discerning eyes of his heart had been washed clean. This inspired me to pray for such a "washing" so that my motives might be realigned with those of my true guide, that I, too, could be redeemed and separated from the "sinister edge" of entanglement and enculturation.

After this prayer, an inner door opened, and into my conscious awareness walked the disheveled John the Baptist, the archetype of the wild man of the "true edge." Here was one who never understated the potency of personal and societal transformation with his graphic imagery of the winnowing fork and the threshing floor and its powerful metaphor of separation: parting wheat from chaff, sifting out what entangles and negatively acculturates us. Unmasking the fear that keeps us from addressing what is real and true about our lives, he beckons us to die as we are plunged beneath the cleansing waters. He then invites us to rise into the sunlight of full wakefulness, attentive to the life before us and open to the *One* who will immerse us in His spirit and transform us with His redeeming and restoring fire.

For a fleeting moment I glimpsed myself standing waist-deep in the river alongside this wild man as he invited me to awaken to what was in front of me, and realign myself with the true guide and his restorative movement in my life. As I sought realignment with my true guide, the words of the consultant psychiatrist came before me, and I was reminded of Christ's strong response to the devil: "Away from me, Satan. For it is written: 'Worship the Lord your God, and serve him only.'"[3] I felt encouraged to hold up my right hand against the sinister entity trying to entangle my motives for guiding Gideon and other pilgrims. I felt a shift within me, and the psychiatrist's words came afresh as an encouragement to do the job I had been gifted to do. I could now acknowledge that Gideon's deepest pulse was already being taken by the Spirit, and that I was in full cooperation with the redeeming and transforming touches of our true guide, the *Holy One* of God.

This encounter with John the Baptist encouraged me to pray that in my own life and in my work with pilgrims, I might be gifted with his clarity and spiritual discernment, his capacity to see through entanglements and mixed motives, his courage to stand on the edge of society rather than close to its center, his willingness to address the winnowing and separation needed in our lives, and his eagerness to serve only his God and to always point pilgrims to the true guide. In bringing these characteristics of John alongside my morning session with Gideon, I could see more clearly how mine was a "dry-land" venture, where I was called to stand waist deep alongside the true guide as he engaged with what was emerging in Gideon, working through the labor of separation towards full redemption. As John bore witness to the true guide, who was both life and light for pilgrims, I trusted that I had reflected to Gideon something of his *way* and that, in speaking words of forgiveness in his name, I had embodied something of his person.

If my time of prayer and reflection that evening had begun with wonderment at what had happened for Gideon that morning, now I was in awe about what had come to reclaim me, having attended to my resonance with Gideon's story and encountered John the Baptist. But I was not quite finished with mystery!

I knew that the pathway we were on as Gideon stepped past his deflated dragon and was redeemed and separated from the "sinister edge" through confession and forgiveness would not guarantee the absence of further pain and suffering, for there were many areas of wounding yet to encounter. I knew that the pathway paved with stepping stones of true light

---

3. Matt 4:10 NRSV.

and life would attract the destructive forces of darkness,[4] for soon after John plunged Jesus beneath the waters of the river, Jesus was pushed into the wilderness to be tested among wild beasts. Then all that was dark and destructive marshaled forces to extinguish the light that had made their treachery visible. And yet, in the face of the enemies of true light and life, and in a physically and emotionally depleted state, Jesus was able to draw clarity, resourcefulness, and strength from something far more powerful: the Word of the living God. "It is written," he replied again and again, and ultimately this caused his tempter to leave him.[5]

In company of this true guide, through the ongoing presence of the Spirit, and with the encouragement of the faith of the great crowd of witnesses who have previously walked this way, Gideon and I can continue down the perilous, wonder-filled pathway of love, grace, mercy, and transformation to full humanity amidst life's wounding, suffering, and joy.

---

4. Matt 5:10 –12.
5. Matt 4:4–11.

Part II:
Sacred Wounds

5

Light Shining in the Darkness

At the beginning of Gideon's fifth visit, I asked what he felt drawn to attend to during our session.

Sitting on the edge of his chair, he said, "Since our last session, I have been paying attention to the things that entangled me. Though I felt freer after realizing I needed forgiveness, I was also very sad. It has been a long time since I have wept so much. While I have not seen 'grief' as clearly as when I was in this room last, 'grief' has certainly been with me. But as I thought about coming today, I felt unsettled, anxious, and sick in my stomach. As I sought to attend to these feelings in prayer this morning, the word *apprehension* stood out. I do feel apprehensive about what I might face today."

"Gideon, can you stay with the unsettled, anxious, feeling sick in the stomach and apprehension?" I asked, aware that what he was experiencing could be preparing him for a significant encounter.

Gideon eased himself into his chair, closed his eyes, and bowed his head. Waiting with him in the silence that followed, I noticed the butterflies in my own stomach. "Lord, have mercy on us," I prayed silently, "and enable me to receive all that might come in your place of rest and calm."

"As I stay with apprehension," Gideon said after a minute, "I'm reminded of a visit I made last year to the worksite of an engineering friend at a huge underground mine. I was anxious about going so deep underground, and my heart was in my mouth as the elevator descended. My anxiety heightened when the lights flickered on and off. My friend noticed my queasy appearance and, to set me at ease, explained that this central part of the mine was just like my tower block inverted underground. His explanation did little to alter my apprehension, for underground, everything seemed distorted."

"You say there was apprehension during this visit to the mine and that underground everything seemed distorted. Can you stay with your apprehension underground and how everything seemed to be distorted?"

Gideon's face creased with concern, and he said, "I feel as if I am moving down into the unknown, coming out of the elevator deep underground. I'm starting to feel sick, and that word *distorted* is gripping me."

"What would it be like to move further down into the unknown, holding onto that word, *distorted*?" I asked.

"I can feel my fear rising. The light is flickering, and everything seems distorted."

"In that place of flickering light and distortion, what are you being invited to do next?" I asked.

"To push against my apprehension and dread and move further into it," Gideon replied, his voice breaking.

"To push against what you have called 'apprehension and dread' and move further into it," I repeated.

"But when I push against the apprehension and dread, I feel something very strong pushing back against me, something like a strong arm shoving me back through the doors of the elevator at the bottom of the mine. It wants me to get back to the surface as quickly as possible, back to familiar territory." Gideon rotated his shoulders, as if trying to free himself from the strong arm.

"As this strong arm tries to force you into that elevator to get you back to familiar territory, what is happening inside?"

"I'm fighting the urge to get back to what is familiar, but I have to use all my courage and strength. Now there's a strong vibration of fear rumbling inside me." Gideon sat upright, pressing his hands against his knees. "This obstacle I'm pressing against, this fear rising up in me—they are fighting me, trying to harm me."

"Fighting you, trying to harm you," I repeated, flinching.

"The whole scene is incredibly dark," Gideon said, his voice rising with panic, "an overwhelming liquid darkness, brimming over with fear and dread."

"A liquid darkness, brimming over with fear and dread," I repeated.

Gideon bent double in his chair. "I dread this darkness and am afraid it will swallow me," he groaned, hiding his face in his hands.

From my quickening heart rate and the weight in my stomach, I intuited that Gideon was on the edge of a major storm.

"Can you stay with this liquid darkness filled with fear and dread?" I asked. In the face of Gideon's panic and distress, I prayed urgently for the restful and calm presence of Jesus. The words "keep him anchored" rose within me.

"The elevator doors have closed behind me, and there is no way out. I feel totally lost in this darkness," Gideon said, opening his panic-filled eyes, pleading for my help.

"You feel lost," I said calmly, casting out a sea anchor to steady Gideon in the midst of the storm we had entered.

"I'm swirling around in this liquid darkness," he sobbed.

As I sought to maintain a calming presence, I felt the waves of panic and anxiety that I knew were swelling over Gideon, as if he were in a flimsy coracle being tossed about on a dark, stormy sea.

Then Gideon clutched at his throat and cried, "The darkness has me by the throat—it's choking me."

The darkness, a rogue wave, had just struck Gideon beam-on and was about to break over the coracle and swamp him. In my mind's eye, I followed the long rope of my imaginary sea anchor and pictured it bringing him bow-about, into the wave. "Gideon, as you notice that the darkness has you by the throat and is choking you, what is it that draws your attention?"

Gideon moved his hands away from his throat and sat motionless and silent, staring before him. Then he looked up at me and said, "This fear that is trying to choke me seems familiar somehow." Then his hands clutched his throat again and the panic returned.

"What do you notice happening to you now?" I asked, trusting my voice to rise above the roar of the wave that had dashed against him.

"It's forcing me down into a dark cavern beneath the mine." Gideon's voice faltered and his eyes filled with terror. "The cavern is filled with freezing water, and it's trying to submerge me."

Pondering the force of this tsunami of fear pulling Gideon into its vortex, I asked, "As you observe yourself being forced into this dark cavern, submerged in freezing water, what do you notice happening next?" Like that sea anchor which serves to steady a ship through a storm without hindering its progress, even though it may be heading off the known course, I hoped my question would guide Gideon back to his observer role without impeding his experience.

"I know I am about to be drowned, yet I am watching in slow motion."

"As you watch in slow motion, can you describe what is happening?"

"I've lost my footing," Gideon said urgently, "and my head is being forced under the water."

"What do you notice as you lose your footing and your head is forced underwater?"

Gideon clutched his chest. "My lungs are about to collapse," he gasped.

"You feel like your lungs are about to collapse. As you struggle to breathe, what do you notice?"

"I'm fighting to get my head above water, and as my head breaches, the water surges up, lifting me with it." Gideon drew a sharp breath and continued. "My lungs are filling with spray and foam."

"As your lungs fill with spray and foam, what else do you notice?"

"The wave has pushed the darkness away. The white spray and foam has brought light."

"What do you see now that it is light?"

"The power of the wave is greater than the darkness."

"As you notice the power of the wave, what happens next?"

"It is washing me to the entrance of the cave instead of throwing me back against the rocks. Now I am sinking like a stone to the depths of the sea."

Aware of the sinking feeling within me, I asked, "As you sink to the depths of the sea, what is happening to you?"

Gideon lapsed into a long silence. Many moments passed before he responded, "This is odd, but I must have drowned, because I've been underwater for some time now." There was surprise in his voice when he next spoke. "But it is completely calm—as if I've entered a different world."

"Can you stay with that experience of calm and that sense of entering a totally different world?"

Gideon relaxed back in his chair, closed his eyes, and bowed his head, his evident calm indicating that the foreign territory he had entered was far from a watery grave. Though I had witnessed Gideon navigating the death of his soul, here was the graced touch of the life-giving Spirit. Before Gideon began to speak, I offered myself in full cooperation with this same Spirit.

"Strange as this may sound," Gideon began, when he finally looked up, "I am beginning to swim—without effort." He paused, then spoke softly, as if his voice might break the spell of this enchanting vision. "I seem to be breathing underwater."

"Though you have drowned, you are swimming and breathing underwater."

Gideon began to explore his new surroundings, describing the floor of the ocean. Then he felt himself drawn toward a light that was "like the sun setting over the water, penetrating the depths of this ocean."

"As you are drawn toward the light that is penetrating the depths of the ocean, what is the light inviting you to do?"

"To swim toward it," he replied.

Gideon then described the experience of swimming upward along a beam of light, which led him to the surface of the water and a sheltered cove. He climbed out of the water and sat on a large smooth rock, warming himself in the sun. After several minutes of calm, he suddenly stirred in his seat.

"What are you noticing as you sit on the rock, warming yourself in the sun?"

"I have just been joined by my parents, and I'm not happy to see them. They have disturbed my peace and my calm. I can feel a knot in my stomach." Gideon paused. "Why am I not pleased to see them?"

"As you ask that question, what do you notice happening to you?"

"The figure of me has become a small boy."

To encourage Gideon to stay with what was emerging before him, I asked, "As you observe the boy with his parents, what draws your attention?"

"The boy wants to show me something that is very important to him."

"Can you invite him to do that?" I asked.

"The images are distorted, and I have to adjust my eyes to see what he is showing me." Gideon paused and closed his eyes.

Intuiting that this meeting with the small boy—the child of his past—would be highly significant, I prayed silently that the Spirit who had guided him to this place of encounter would enlighten the eyes of his heart.

"I can see that we are back in the family home, where he is making sure his room is tidy and vacuuming the floors. Now he's doing homework. But the little boy seems to be in such a hurry. Now he's tiptoeing past his father's study so he doesn't disturb him, then hurrying outside to pull weeds out of the garden. The closer I look, the more frantic he seems to be. Oh no!" Gideon exclaimed. "He has just knocked over a flower pot with the wheelbarrow, and the clatter brings father to the window. He does not seem to be pleased, and I can feel the child wince as his eyes meet his father's. It's a wince tinged with fear."

"Gideon, just as you experience the wince tinged with fear, what more do you notice occurring within this little boy?"

In the silence that followed, Gideon became distressed, and I could see that he was on the verge of tears. A lump formed in my own throat.

"I can feel desperation welling up inside," he said as the tears began to flow. "Inside, the little boy is frantic."

"What do you notice about the desperation welling up in you and the little boy's franticness?" I asked, my eyes stinging with tears.

"The little boy is desperately afraid that his parents—our parents—will abandon him. And that same desperation is present within me as well. My father did leave my mother and me when I was eight, but even as I say that, it doesn't extinguish the fear that has continued to push me into frantic activity."

"As you stay with the desperation and fear, what do you notice happening for the little boy?"

"He has to stop them from leaving him," Gideon replied. "As I come closer, there seems to be a flood of jumbled thoughts, fears, and sadness locked inside us."

"Can you slow down that flood and lay out those thoughts, fears, and sadness before you?" I asked, realizing that Gideon was struggling to stay with the distress emanating from the little boy's heart.

"That seems to be happening, almost as if those thoughts and fears have become white powder and are settling in the dust before me as words and phrases: 'If you don't please your parents they will leave you!' 'That will be your punishment!' 'It is you who have caused all of this!' 'They fight each other because of you!' 'You have to work for their love!' 'If they leave you there will be no one to care for you and you will die!' The others are too blurred to read." Gideon buried his head in his hands. "This is too much," he sobbed.

"You are saying this is too much."

"It's too much for such a little boy to carry. It's breaking his heart." Gideon began to sob.

I waited until the sobbing abated, then said, "When you feel the time is right, I wonder if you could bring your gaze to your parents?"

When Gideon finally spoke, there was a tinge of anger in his voice. "I don't want to look at them," he said, then added, "how could they do that to such a small defenseless boy?"

"You are asking, 'How could they do that to this little boy?' I wonder what it would be like to place that question in front of the boy and his parents, as if it were written in white powder on the ground between them."

Gideon said that his parents had moved aside, out of earshot of the boy. They were deep in conversation, perhaps an argument. He listened in as best he could, catching only small fragments, noticing how they were becoming more conflicted and less attentive to each other.

Suddenly Gideon looked directly into my eyes. "It's not the boy they are talking about leaving!" he stammered. "It's each other. The boy believes that the conflict between them is his fault!"

Gideon slumped back in his chair, exhausted from this encounter. I felt both relief and grief, yet I intuited that this journey had not yet ended. As the anchor man, it was my job to extend calm and safety so that Gideon could remain silently attentive to what was emerging in front of him.

"Just for a fleeting moment," Gideon began, breaking the silence, "I was back on that road I walked upon in one of our earlier sessions, hearing those unsettling cries from the darkness. One of the emotions journeying along the road has escaped from the rest and, like a fugitive, is lurking in the undergrowth close by the road."

Though momentarily jolted by this shift in Gideon's focus, I reminded myself that the Spirit was enlivening the eyes of Gideon's heart.

Then Gideon spoke slowly and deliberately, "The fugitive is the little boy's 'abandonment,' who has been held captive all these years, a prisoner deep in the cavern beneath the mine." Gideon paused to take a deep breath. "Held captive in the dark, the little boy's abandonment has become distorted. Before today, if I even came close to such a feeling, it was like being forced into that mine elevator and then hurrying to the surface, desperate to get back to familiar territory as quickly as possible. How that has driven me through my life! But that wave brought this fugitive out of the darkness to the surface, into the light of day—what an incredible journey!"

"In this 'incredible journey' of bringing the fugitive out of captivity, out of distortion into the light, what do you notice about 'abandonment' now?"

"I see my adult self back on that road. As you said the word *abandonment*, she came out of the brush, and she is walking along the road beside me as a friend—not an enemy who wants to harm me."

"As you notice 'abandonment' as your friend, I am wondering if your parents are still in the picture."

I could see the lightness that had accompanied the naming and freeing of "abandonment" give way to a darker brooding.

"Yes, and they are still arguing," he said with sorrow. "But as they notice the figure of the little boy, they stop arguing. My mother is crying, and my father doesn't seem to know what to do or say—that's unusual, as he usually seems so sure of himself."

"Can you see your mother's face?" I asked.

"I am looking into it now, and she just said, 'What is to become of my precious little boy?'" Gideon looked away and was silent for some time.

"Can you stay with her face?"

When he looked up, his eyes were full of tears. "Her heart is breaking for me. They aren't leaving me—the conflict is between them. They are arguing about their separation. All these years, the little boy believed in his broken heart that they were leaving because of him, but that was not true. It was a lie!"

Gideon's eyelids flickered as if to refocus his vision.

"What are you noticing?" I asked, intuiting by his sorrowful expression that he was facing even more pain.

"In my mother's eyes," he gasped, "I see 'abandonment,' a fugitive held captive deep within her, in that place beneath the mine." Gideon began to weep. When he lifted his face, there was a pleading look in his eyes. "What was tragic for the little boy was even more tragic for my mother. She was adopted and has never been able to trace her birth mother. Until this very moment, I have never been aware of her abandonment."

"You are saying that what was tragic for the little boy was even more tragic for your mother, and you are now aware of her abandonment. If you bring your gaze back to the little boy, what do you notice about him?"

"Some of the abandonment he carried was mixed with his mother's. The word *distorted* comes back to me. When it was all mixed together, it became distorted, confused and dark. Now, as it becomes clearer, it was tragic for my mother and a heavy burden for a little boy to carry locked up in his heart."

Gideon sighed, then added, "What incredible relief for me, but what great sadness for my mother." His relief, mingled with sadness, resonated with what I was feeling.

During the long silence that followed, I felt the holiness of Gideon communing with God—a holiness so palpable I felt stirred to take off my shoes, but I did not want to disturb his peace.

When Gideon finally broke the silence, he said, "It might seem bold to say this, but I believe God has been in this place. I am thinking of that psalm about God's Spirit being in the heavens and the depths."

I reached for the Bible and found this reference in the Psalms.[6] We both spoke out these verses as our benediction:

> Where can I go from your spirit?
> Or where can I flee from your presence?
> If I ascend to heaven, you are there;
> if I make my bed in Sheol, you are there.
> If I take the wings of the morning
> and settle at the farthest limits of the sea,
> even there your hand shall lead me,
> and your right hand shall hold me fast.
> If I say, "Surely the darkness shall cover me,
> and the light around me become night,"
> even the darkness is not dark to you;
> the night is as bright as the day,
> for darkness is as light to you.

"Thanks be to God."

"Thanks be to God, indeed," Gideon said, "and I must also hold that hope for my mother."

---

6. Ps 139: 7–12 NRSV.

6

From Death to New Life

A meeting that evening restricted my time for prayer and reflection, but what remained with me from my session with Gideon hovered in my consciousness, waiting for time and space to settle and reveal its treasures. My nightfall reading from the Psalms spoke of God's desire to teach us wisdom and to find truth in the depths of our soul,[1] which resonated with the journey Gideon and I had taken earlier that day. In the moments of pondering prior to sleep, I was amazed by how the Spirit of God had been manifest throughout this encounter, intertwining with Gideon's spirit to bring about transformation deep within his soul. I felt awe at how the Spirit had entered Gideon's stories, metaphors, and emotions, awakened him to the truth of his wounding, and offered him greater interior freedom.

God's Spirit continues to instruct our hearts during sleep,[2] and that night I was given a vivid dream. As I ventured along a pathway, I found my way barred by a huge spiderweb. My first thought was that the web could have easily entangled me, making me prey, but this fear evaporated as my gaze was captured by tiny dewdrops, each highlighted by the sun's rays, displaying an array of exquisite gems. I stood mesmerized by the transfigured dewdrops as the web was slowly eclipsed by darkness, then reconfigured in the bluish hue of the rising moon.

As a refreshing breeze gently lifted the web, it became a labyrinth filled with intricate passageways, and each dewdrop became a tiny capsule

1. Ps 51:6.
2. Ps 16:7.

carrying a message to the center of the web from its edges and back again. Captivated by the living form and flow of this spectacle, I didn't realize at first that sections of the web were torn, and the traffic of capsules was congested in these regions. As I studied these marred sections, the largest shriveled and fell away. But then a golden light began moving through the torn passages, enabling the capsules to move freely again.

When I awoke, I carried into my consciousness the awareness of these vivid web and labyrinth images, along with feelings of rejoicing mingled with overwhelming pain and sorrow.

Wanting to extend prayerful attentiveness to this dream metaphor and the emotions that accompanied my waking, I took time to contemplate both my emotions and the content of my dream so that I would not become distracted by my morning routine or the demands of my day.

As I held the contradictory emotions of joy and sorrow, I thought of the joys, pains, and sorrows Gideon experienced as he was guided deep within his soul to places of wounding, distortion, and entanglement so that the pain of his abandonment could be transformed into a treasure of newfound freedom. Guided by the truth-seeking light of the Spirit, messengers had invited Gideon to visit the inner archives of his soul, bringing to conscious awareness the truth of his lived experience—including the site of his wounding, where the distortion of life events had led to captivity and entanglement. Through this movement of transformation, the wound had become a sacred doorway into the holiness of God.

Slowly shifting my focus from Gideon's experience back to my dream, I reflected on the labyrinth as a metaphor for the *form* of the human soul, with the ceaseless *flow* of capsules through its passages as a symbol of the human spirit. I wondered if I was being offered a privileged glimpse of the labyrinth of Gideon's soul, with its exquisite passages flowing with inner messengers, giving and receiving, bearing both beauty and fragility.

This metaphor for our interior life continued to grow within my imagination as I realized that the labyrinth had both center and periphery, with intricate passageways not unlike our arteries and veins, all carrying different types of blood, with capillaries serving memory archives and deposits of truth and wisdom. Not only do these archives contain thoughts of what we have been doing and what has occurred to us, but also what God has been doing and what has occurred between God and us.

At the periphery, the place where our spirits actively engage the actions and relationships of our external world, I could see that all those actions and relationships of daily life were flowing toward the center of the web. For when we delve beneath the surface of our daily lives, God's Spirit guides us to journey deeper into the labyrinth of our soul. From this hub of intimate encounter with our Creator God, we re-emerge at the periphery of the labyrinth filled with wonder and gratitude for the reciprocal flow of giving and receiving with God and with God's creation. As I meditated on this metaphor, I was filled with vibrancy, freedom, and an overflowing sensation of life. I remembered Irenaeus' insight that "the glory of God is man fully alive" and heard the words of Jesus, reminding me that his yoke is easy and his burden is light.[3]

As I basked in these refreshing words and images, the earlier feelings of pain and sorrow began to mingle with the joy of lightness, freedom, and life. I could not escape the tragic reality of the marred segments of the web, nor could I shake free of the sorrow that the surpassing merit of the soul's intricate design, bearing as it does the imprint of the Creator, so often goes unacknowledged. The dream had revealed the tenuous connection of these entangled segments with the more intact parts of the web, and I had seen one segment shrivel and die. As I lingered with these painful images, the memory of Gideon's struggle resurfaced. I recalled his courage in resisting the temptation to return to familiar territory and his willingness to face the darkness within. I remembered the power stronger than darkness that had led him to the depths of the ocean to the experience of drowning. Feeling the pain and sorrow well up within me again, I felt stirred to keep watch and pray at these portals of death—the dying segment of the web, Gideon's experience of drowning, and his encounter of the small boy and his parents.

As I watched and prayed, I experienced anew my recent journey through Holy Week, when I had walked—along with several others in my community of faith—in solidarity with Jesus as friend, brother, and Lord through the story of his Passion. Early in Holy Week, we prepared through prayer, scripture reading, and silence. Thursday night, we were invited to stay, watch, wait, and pray with Jesus in the turmoil and agony of the garden, remaining attentive to our own distractedness and weariness. We stood near Jesus through his trial, stood next to the women through his crucifixion, listened intently to his cry of forsakenness and the words he uttered as he gave up his spirit: "It is finished." We asked ourselves if we could carry Jesus' death in our own bodies. The tears ran freely down our

---

3. Matt 11:30.

cheeks as we sang, "Did e'er such love and sorrow meet, or thorns compose so rich a crown?"[4]

From this point, I figured we would leave this place of sorrow and look forward to Sunday's shouts of "Christ is risen; He is risen indeed!" But on Saturday night, we were invited to withhold the possibility of the resurrection until it actually came upon us with newness and surprise on Easter Sunday.

I found this last request to be the hardest, for this is where we experience the high cost of restoration and transformation. And yet, as I pondered this Holy Week journey again in the context of my dream and journey with Gideon, I realized that my engagement with Jesus' Passion had extended my capacity to wait, watch, and pray amidst darkness and deathlike experiences long enough to ponder the question of what needs to die so that the Spirit might raise this young pilgrim to new and abundant life. To make this journey, I had to hold back my speculations so that the mysterious light of the Spirit could course through the entanglement of the shriveled and dead parts of the labyrinth and bring new life, reconnecting its periphery to its center.

As I pondered the significant turning points in Gideon's journey, Jesus' Passion was mirrored back to me. I saw Gideon's dying in the metaphor of drowning, his being raised to new life in the ability to breathe underwater, and his discovery of deeper and liberating truth in the encounter with his parents and the unmasking of abandonment. I saw in Gideon's encounter with the Spirit a love far more embracing and self-giving than the conditional love that had led to his relational wounding, a love far greater than the love that had faded between his parents or the love between his mother and him, which had been so distorted by his mother's experience of abandonment. The love he encountered was strong enough to pull together the fragments of his fragile human soul, resilient enough to embrace his cries of abandonment and forsakenness, and far-reaching enough to bridge life and death. My own Holy Week experience of waiting for Jesus' resurrection enveloped me in joyful and astonished surprise when I witnessed the Spirit's restorative and transforming work within Gideon.

As I came to the end of this morning time of prayer and reflection, my inner gaze shifted back to the boy Gideon and the abandonment that for more than twenty-five years had been held captive and distorted in a hidden and tangled segment of his soul's labyrinth.

4. Watts, "When I Survey the Wondrous Cross."

But then my gaze shifted to my own interior, and I realized how quickly I neglect my Creator's imprint, whose essence and unity is so intricately woven into the labyrinth of my soul. As this metaphor took hold of me, my heart burned within me, delivering me to the open portal of the *form* of the Trinity—Father, Son, and Holy Spirit—and their endless *flow* of self-giving, other-receiving and sacrificial love, a love that flowed freely through me to Gideon. And I realized, with great surprise, that on the breath of the same Spirit it was flowing back from Gideon to me.

7

A Touch from Above

A fortnight later, Gideon began our sixth session by describing how his attention had been continuously drawn back to himself as a six-year-old boy. "Because of my fear, I have neglected him over these years—actually locked him away in an inaccessible place. But during our last session, God broke down the door and released him from that dungeon. Now here he is, right with me."

"What happens to you when you realize the little boy has been released and is right with you?"

Gideon pondered my question. "By being present, he is making my childhood more available to me. But even with this new freedom, I still have mixed emotions and many unanswered questions."

"You still have mixed emotions and many unanswered questions," I repeated. "Can you say more about the emotions you are experiencing?"

"I'm not afraid of this gutsy little survivor now that I have met him. But I do feel sad for him and sometimes angry over what he went through. I think I feel compassionate as well, yet I'm afraid that he will expose me to more sorrow and hurt." Gideon looked at me. "You know me well enough to know I run from pain. But I can't run anymore, because I know there's nowhere to hide." Gideon paused. "And I can't blame my mother after seeing what she went through."

"When you say that you can't run anymore because there is nowhere to hide, and that you can't blame your mother, what happens with your compassion for the little boy?"

Gideon shut his eyes, and I imagined him holding a little boy within his compassionate adult gaze. A feeling of relief welled up within me as I realized that at last there was a loving adult who might be able to understand the lost little boy.

As I imagined this scene, Gideon began to weep. When he spoke at last, his voice was soft and tender. "You know, Julian, he just needs someone to accept him, to approve of him, to love him just the way he is."

"To accept him, to approve of him, to love him just the way he is," I repeated, feeling as I said these words an intensification of the relief I had felt moments before. After several moments of silence, I asked where this acceptance, approval, and love might be found.

"From my parents, I wish," he said flatly.

Intuiting Gideon's disappointment, I summoned the courage to ask, "Are they able to do it for him?"

Gideon took a long time to respond, and I wondered if he was hoping for a miracle, that he might see his parents respond in an accepting and loving way. "My father does not seem to know how to respond. And my mother"—his voice faltered—"seems to have this brittle shell around her body. I know she loves the little boy, but her own pain and abandonment have shut her down. She seems to be functioning like a robot." After another long pause, he concluded, "No, I do not believe either of them can give the little boy the love he so desperately needs."

I prayerfully pondered my next question, wanting to keep Gideon attentive to this little boy while inwardly acknowledging that I was walking on a delicate edge. "Is there someone else who might be able to do it?" I inquired tentatively.

"Granny could!" he exclaimed.

Thank you, God, for Granny, I prayed inwardly, as outwardly I asked, "Does she come?"

"Yes, but then she has to go away, and the little boy is sad again."

I realized that I had to proceed in hope, the hope beyond hope of the resurrection—and that hope was my lifeline as I asked the next question. "Who else could accept, approve of, and love this little boy just the way he is?"

Gideon seemed to be moved, and then he said, "No, there is no one." After another long pause, he said, "Only God!"

Inwardly, I greeted his response with surprise and joy, for here was another resurrection. Thanking God in my spirit, I asked, "What would it be like to invite God to come and respond to this sad little boy?"

While I knew I needed to trust the story thread emerging for Gideon, I also knew that moving across such a threshold could cause some pilgrims to panic. But Gideon's response came from a place of real trust in the manifest presence of the true guide.

As the little boy encountered Jesus, the adult Gideon observed, "Jesus is welcoming the little boy with obvious compassion, but the little boy is cautious, even resistant."

"There is welcome and compassion from Jesus, but the little boy is cautious and resistant," I repeated. "Without intruding on the little boy, might you encourage him to direct his concerns, resistance, and questions to Jesus?"

"I'm not sure," Gideon replied with a quizzical look on his face.

"Does the little boy see you observing him?" I asked.

"Why, now he does—and I can encourage him to do as you suggested."

During the silence that followed, Gideon looked startled, then sad.

"The little boy," he began hesitantly, "has asked Jesus why he did not come to him when he felt abandoned and lost."

As Gideon shared this observation, I felt a sharp inner pain and the heat of tears pressing against my eyes. "What do you notice Jesus doing?" I asked quietly, not wanting to intrude on this encounter.

"He is weeping," Gideon said.

I waited for a moment, then asked, "As you notice Jesus' weeping, what begins to happen to you?"

"I can feel his sadness mixing with my own."

Gideon leaned back in his chair with his eyes closed and his chin against his chest. I felt momentarily paralyzed as I sensed that Gideon and I had just been offered a tiny glimpse into the great grief of God.

"It is very strange," Gideon said slowly, as if unable to find the right words. "Jesus is in here." He pointed to the lower region of his stomach. "And I realize he was there all the time."

"As you realize he was there when you felt abandoned and lost, what happens next?"

"The little boy has moved into Jesus' arms and is resting with his head on Jesus' chest." With relief and surprise, Gideon added, "I think he's gone to sleep!"

As Gideon pondered this scene, I felt amazed by the gift of watching this little boy become reconciled to Jesus. By reaching deep into his inner treasure trove to pull out the gem of trust, Gideon had found in Christ the acceptance and love he had been searching for much of his life.

I waited in the silence until Gideon looked up. "What have you been noticing?" I asked.

"I've been watching the little boy as he sleeps in Jesus' arms." Gideon sighed. "I've never witnessed such love and acceptance."

"And as you witness that love and acceptance, what is happening for you?"

"Just as you said that, the little boy woke up, and he's noticed me and is smiling at me. Jesus is as well." Gideon paused and his voice trembled. "They are beckoning me to join them."

"What do you choose to do?"

"I hesitate. I'm just not sure!"

"Can you take a moment to notice your hesitation and your not being sure?"

"You would think that with all the healing I have experienced I would join them immediately."

"Do you notice anything standing in the space between you and Jesus and the little boy?"

"There's a roadblock—like one of those 'Detour' or 'Diversion' signs."

"Detour or diversion," I repeated.

Gideon sighed. "As I look at Jesus and the little boy, I know they are beckoning me to come into a committed relationship. I know that, deep down, I want and need that." Gideon hesitated, then added, "But that's scary, and I'm much more adept at looking for a diversion."

"On the one hand," I said, holding out my left hand, "there is an invitation into a committed relationship, and you know you want and need that. But on the other hand," I continued, holding out my right hand, "you say it would be scary and that you are much better looking for a diversion." Holding my left hand out to Gideon, I said, "Now, take a moment to move your gaze from the invitation to a committed relationship and"—indicating with my right hand—"the feeling of being scared and looking for a diversion."

"Over the past few weeks, I've realized how strongly I have resisted looking at my childhood all these years. And I know that the fear of facing that pain has been taken away by Jesus, who is beckoning to me now. But real commitment to relationship with a person is just too scary. You know,

Julian, I'm just about to lose a relationship with my girlfriend, Judith, because she is looking for a long-term commitment—and I just can't do that."

"As you have been saying that out loud, Gideon, what do you notice about Jesus?"

Gideon bit his bottom lip. "He is saying he knows and understands and that it is okay." His voice trembled as he continued. "He is also saying that he can deal with the feelings of guilt and shame that I carry over all of that."

Gideon glanced at me with a pleading look on his face. "But how do I know that is true?"

"As you ask that question, what does Jesus do?"

Gideon rocked in his chair and said in a muffled voice, "He is holding out his hands, just like you did before."

"And what do you notice about his hands as he holds them out to you?"

"They are wounded!"

Gideon ceased rocking and settled back in his chair, tears flowing down his face. From the warmth burning within me, I knew that Gideon was experiencing the real and manifest presence of Jesus.

After several minutes, Gideon said, "I finally joined them, ready for some conversation about commitment, guilt, and shame, but the little boy was so playful, and so Jesus and I joined in a game with him. It was such fun, but strangely I also felt sorrow that I could not recall ever having such a time of free abandonment in play. Then the little boy seemed to disappear, but I realized after a while that it was as if he had reentered my body, and the distinctness between me as the adult and the little boy evaporated. Then Jesus lit a fire, and we sat together, with our feet to the fire, talking heart to heart without the need of words."

Gideon grinned. "I just said we sat with our feet to the fire—how about that! That's what people say to young men: 'When are you going to put your feet to the fire?' Commitment without diversion! Have I just been drawn into it?"

"Is that what's happened to you, Gideon?"

"Yes, because I had the freedom to choose it—just like the freedom of our play, with no one looking over our shoulders asking 'what if' questions, no guilt, no shame. There is just this profound sense of being loved and accepted for who I am."

In the presence of Jesus, Gideon was embraced and warmed by the redeeming and restorative love that flows from the very heart of the triune God. "Something became alive within me," he explained, "and I knew that in spite of my childhood, I was and am profoundly loved and accepted. When I finally let go of what I had craved for so long, this *greater love* found me." He paused. "You know, I was going to add that I had also found approval, but I discovered much more than that—I realized that I was and am desired!" Gideon sighed. "I'm so, so grateful."

In the holy silence that followed, both Gideon and I, pilgrim and guide, encountered God. Gideon ended the session by saying, "Amen."

"Amen," I responded.

8

Full of Grace and Truth

Before settling into my time of evening prayer and reflection, I thought about how Gideon, a gifted engineer, had responded to the call of his neglected interior and wounded heart. The construction metaphor that had captured his imagination a fortnight earlier had been of a tower inverted underground above a watery cavern, beyond which was the deep ocean that had claimed him. My mind wandered to one of my few constructions—putting together a tiny wooden sailing dinghy from a pre-cut kit. When I questioned my accuracy with part of this task, someone quipped that the engineer works within a thousandth of an inch, the carpenter an eighth, but a boatbuilder is glad to be on the correct boat. Though psychology can tell us much about the construction of our personality and wounding, the healing of the human heart is never a precise enterprise.

Looking back on today's session, I was amazed by the way that Gideon—a highly intelligent, creative young man who had been able to conjure up a finished building in his imagination—had engaged with a different kind of workmanship. He had let himself be drawn into relationship with a man of roughly his own age, whose mind, heart, and spirit could hold the unified Gideon in his imagination and mediate that restored image, little by little, through their time together.

In the prologue to his Gospel, John spoke of us seeing "the glory of the One and Only, who came from the Father, full of grace and truth,"[1] and this is what both Gideon and I experienced earlier when we witnessed

---

1. John 1:14 NIV.

the manifest presence of Jesus speaking directly to Gideon's heart to bring about his profound healing and restoration.

During my prayer and reflection, I was drawn to sit in silence with my own wounded and fragmented self before the mind, heart, and spirit of the Lord. When thoughts knocked noisily at the edges of my consciousness, I welcomed and farewelled them, gently spoke the name of Jesus, and returned to be present to him. As I emerged from the silence later, I realized that the truth and grace that Gideon had experienced that morning was also a gift for me.

As I pondered that gift, my attention was drawn back to 2 Peter, which had been my evening scripture reading: "Everything that goes into a life of pleasing God has been miraculously given to us by getting to know, personally and intimately, the One who invited us to God. The best invitation we ever received!"[2] I had been both witness to and recipient of that miraculous gift, and this realization filled me with gratitude and awe.

As I remembered the encounter I had witnessed between Gideon and Jesus, my attention was drawn to the moment when Jesus beckoned the adult Gideon to join him and the little boy. Gideon had been able to name how his avoidance of commitment had diverted him from intimate relationships—including with his girlfriend, Judith—and he could see that this was the roadblock between Jesus and him. I could see how grace had revealed the truth of this roadblock, which had been constructed by Gideon's relational wounding and was encased in guilt and shame. At the same time, Gideon was able to see the heart-wrenching image of the grief and love that had won the heart of the lost little boy. With outstretched, wounded hands, Jesus released the adult Gideon from his fear, isolation, guilt, and shame. In this movement I witnessed the intermingling of Jesus' grace and truth, as described in the first chapter of John. I could also see how getting to know Jesus intimately had revealed significant truths about my own life, bringing me home to who I am by grace and offering me greater freedom to embrace myself as well as others around me.

As I contemplated this image of Jesus reaching out to me, a significant prelude to today's healing began to open before me. I remembered the character, "grief," who in an earlier session had offered to accompany Gideon on his journey of awakening and discovery, knowing the part it could play in his legitimate experience of pain and suffering. I remembered Gideon's painful drowning and resurrection and how this enabled the little

---

2. 2 Pet 1:3 MSG.

boy within him to be released from captivity. I remembered the encounter between the little boy and his parents, when Gideon discovered his own experience of abandonment and grew to understand his mother's wounding. I remembered Gideon's growing concern, compassion, grief, and even anger for the lost little boy of his childhood. I saw how important it had been for the little boy to feel safe, to experience love and acceptance, to know that he had not caused his parent's separation, and to have the truth of his experiences acknowledged and validated by his adult counterpart. More than ever, I could see how important it was for the little boy, who represented Gideon's lost childhood, to be honored and grieved over.

I saw with renewed wonder how the touch of Jesus rests upon what is deeply human—the truth of our lived experiences—and how the miraculous does not circumvent pain and grief but rather leads us through it. I felt Jesus speaking to me: "See how Gideon's faith, encouraged by your own faith, contributes to making him whole!"

As I acknowledged this with gratitude, I began to experience the warmth and tenderness of Jesus in welcoming the little boy, his grief over him, and the gentle arms that had enfolded this child, bringing him to a place of rest. Awakening to the truth of his experiences had been significant for Gideon's healing, but so had the grace, acceptance, and rest through Jesus' tenderness and love. I knew that this balance of grace and truth was what I most needed in my guiding of pilgrims.

In my experience of Jesus' total acceptance, warmth, and tenderness, my imagination drew me to the way Jesus brought troubled pilgrims such as Gideon into the presence of his "Abba-Father." Though Gideon had not described this image of Jesus, I saw Jesus' wounded hands lifting the child Gideon up to his Father.

As I meditated on this image, I found myself lifting cupped hands in such a gesture, and I remembered the near weightless body of a tiny, wounded bird I had lifted from the roadway a few evenings before. I could feel my hands cupping the fluttering clump of bones and feathers against my chest, knowing that if I held the bird too tightly she would be crushed, and if I loosened my grasp she might fall to her death.

As I held the image of this tiny bird alongside the picture of Jesus lifting up the child of Gideon, my attention was drawn back to the wounded hands of Christ offering us grace with one hand and truth with the other. As I pictured myself restoring the tiny bird to its nest in the tree above the roadway, I heard Jesus' grief in his lament over Jerusalem: "How often I have desired to gather your children together as a hen gathers her brood under her wings, and you were not willing! See your house is left to you, desolate."[3]

I do not want to see pilgrims such as Gideon left desolate but long to stand with them at thresholds adjacent to their grief and desolation, reflecting back to them the grace and truth of the One "who comes in the name of the Lord,"[4] bringing them close to the heart from whose fullness and generosity pilgrims receive "grace upon grace."[5] This longing resonated with my vocational desire to companion pilgrims in the way of the true guide and to reflect, however dimly, the same self-giving, other-receiving and sacrificial love that could only flow from the heart of the community of the Trinity.

As my thoughts returned to Gideon and the truth and grace he had experienced, I wondered what other shifts might occur as he began to come home to himself and his Lord in the weeks ahead.

---

3. Matt 23:37–38 NRSV.
4. Matt 23:39 NRSV.
5. John 1:16 NRSV.

Part III: Restoration

9

Initiation into New Life

When I met Gideon for his seventh session, I asked where he wanted to begin our time together.

"Over the past few days, the word *initiation* has been coming to me. I know adolescent men in different cultures undergo initiation ceremonies, but it makes me think of young people performing antisocial acts to become part of a gang. Yet during prayer, *initiation* keeps coming, so I know it must have significance."

"As the word *initiation* kept coming, what began to happen for you?"

"Last night, when I took *initiation* to God in prayer, I felt guided toward the story of Jesus' baptism." He paused and looked at me with a grin. "You know, Julian, your encouragement these past months to attend to what is emerging in front of me kept me with the story. I went back to the account in Matthew's Gospel and consulted a commentary. But I'm not sure what to do next."

"Gideon, as you come to the question of what to do next with the story of Jesus' baptism, what begins to happen?"

"I'm intrigued by this event in Jesus' life, but I'm confused about what it might have to do with me. I've already been baptized."

"Intrigued, baffled," I repeated back.

"During our last visit, I saw the abandoned boy of my childhood find real love and acceptance in the presence of Jesus—that was an incredible shift for me. But why am I finding all this energy around the story of his baptism?" As Gideon said "why," he held out the upturned palms of his hands.

Mirroring Gideon's gesture of opening his hands, I raised my left hand and said, "Last time we met, the abandoned boy found real love and acceptance in the presence of Jesus." Then I raised my right hand and continued, "You have noticed an inner shift, and the word *initiation* and the story of Jesus' baptism have become important to you."

Gideon's gaze moved from one of my open hands to the other. "In baptism, Jesus is being initiated into his particular vocation of life and faith. And I am being initiated into my unique vocation of life and faith. What is happening to Jesus is somehow happening to me!"

Gideon's demeanor conveyed amazement, and as he spent time savoring this new epiphany, I felt the thrill of the Spirit's insight.

When Gideon looked up, I reflected back his new insight. "You have noticed two stories of initiation—your own and the initiation of Jesus. What happens as you spend time with these two stories?"

"Because I just spent time with Matthew's account of Jesus' baptism, I can see it unfolding right in front of me—as if I am one of the onlookers."

"You can see Jesus' baptism unfold in front of you, and you are one of the onlookers," I responded.

"I am looking at Jesus, who is about my age. He is standing with his friends under a tree near a riverbank. His attention is focused on an unkempt man, who must be John the Baptist, standing waist-deep in water. But what is Jesus doing?"

"What do you notice Jesus doing?" I asked, echoing back Gideon's question.

"His face is lifted toward heaven with his eyes closed, and his whole body is shuddering. Now he is walking toward the muddy water. The air around him feels heavy, as if he is walking toward danger or something that will challenge him. John, who is tall, strong, and powerful, is hesitating as Jesus plunges waist-deep into the water before him. Jesus insists, so John lowers him beneath the waters of the river. As Jesus rises up out of the water, a shimmering whiteness in the shape of a dove descends upon him."

I gave Gideon time to absorb what he had witnessed, watching his upper body rock gently back and forth.

Following an intuition that Gideon might move closer to the person of Jesus, when he opened his eyes, I asked, "As you stand as an onlooker at Jesus' baptism, I wonder if Jesus notices you there?"

"He is beckoning to me to join him and John in the river, just as he invited the little boy to come to him in our last session. He seems to be inviting me to be baptized by John."

Gideon fell silent. As I contemplated what might be happening for him, his countenance changed, and he began to look very perturbed.

"What are you beginning to notice?" I asked gently.

"The water is very cold and it is right up to my neck."

He seemed distressed, so I reflected back, "You notice the water is cold and it is up to your neck."

Gideon gasped, "I am back in the waterhole at the bottom of the dark cavern!"

I had not anticipated this sudden twist in Gideon's story, but I reminded myself that my role as guide was to keep Gideon attentive to what was emerging in front of him, however sinister or surprising.

"You are back in the waterhole of the dark cavern," I said calmly. "What are you noticing in that place?"

"The water is freezing cold. It is so familiar—I hate it."

To encourage his attentiveness I repeated, "The water is cold and familiar and you hate it. What do you notice next?"

"I feel as if I am facing death again. But I have been through all this before."

"You feel as if you are facing death again, but you have been through this before."

"It feels like death, but I know I'm not dying, because I can breathe underwater."

"As you experience what feels like dying, but you know is not dying, what happens next?"

"I see myself back at the river with Jesus and John."

"As you see yourself back at the river with Jesus and John, what do you notice?"

"The water is warm. The sun is shining. I can breathe freely again. I feel very safe."

I could see that Gideon was experiencing something more, so I asked, "What are you noticing now?"

"There is a heaviness around my shoulders, a huge weight, like something I have brought with me from the dark cavern."

"What do you notice about this weight on your shoulders?"

"I can see it now," replied Gideon. "It is full of those past strivings to get things right, my poor choices, sadness about my family and the ways I responded to them, my own self-serving. As I notice more and more, the weight is pushing me down into the river. So many things have been weighing me down, holding me back." Gideon rolled his shoulders, as if to shrug off his burden.

"As the weight of all of this presses you down into the river, what happens next?"

"John is lowering me beneath the water."

"As he does that, what begins to happen?"

"The weight I was carrying is being washed away by the water. I am not struggling, but am calm and relaxed."

Watching Gideon breathe normally, I waited before reflecting back, "The things that have been weighing you down have been washed away, and you are very calm and relaxed."

"John is bringing me up out of the water, and everything seems bathed in light. I am looking back to John to thank him, but he is urging me to join Jesus and follow him."

"He is urging you to join and follow Jesus. What do you choose to do?"

"I feel a great sense of freedom in making that choice."

"What do you do with that freedom?"

"I choose . . ." he said quietly, then added with conviction, "I choose to become a follower of the One who has offered me so much love and acceptance and who has revealed to me that I am desirable in God's sight. I choose to be initiated into his way!"

Having already learned from John, whom this young pilgrim had called "unkempt," that I was to decrease in order to allow Jesus, the true guide, to increase, I knew not to express my complete joy and amazement directly to Gideon. But joy, amazement, and gratitude did follow me through the day as I looked forward to my time of reflection and prayer that evening.

10

On Earth as in Heaven

Having been a witness to the interweaving of Jesus' baptism with Gideon's initiation into Jesus' life, the joy, amazement, and gratitude that accompanied me into my evening time of prayer and reflection drew from the deep waters of redemption and transformation.[1] Even as I allowed these thoughts to wash over me, I became aware that Gideon's formation as a human being had involved his dying and rising with Christ.[2] He had responded to a personal invitation to participate more deeply in the life that Jesus refers to as "the kingdom of God."

During the morning's session, I had witnessed the Spirit's revelation in Gideon's life, and this epiphany had resonated deeply within my own soul. In my time of prayer and reflection, I felt urged to ponder the richness of this revelation, to catch it as I might a ball. Cupping my hands as if to hold such a ball, it seemed to bounce at the edge of my conscious awareness, bringing with it two phrases from the Lord's Prayer: "Thy kingdom come. Thy will be done in earth, as it is in heaven."[3]

As I inwardly repeated this prayer over and over, I wondered if I had caught a glimpse of the kingdom manifesting itself on earth as in heaven. I had caught a glimpse of Gideon being initiated into the life of the kingdom. I had seen a significant movement in Gideon's personal and spiritual formation, which was also reflective of what might be done in heaven. Gideon

1. Isa 12:3.
2. Rom 6:4.
3. Matt 6:10 KJV.

was being formed in the likeness of Jesus, and for a fleeting moment, I had seen in his unveiled face a tiny reflection of the Lord's glory.

I knew that my strength—the strength of my work as a guide—was in the joy of the Lord.[4] By cooperating with the Spirit, I had been invited to share in the joy of Gideon being transformed on earth as in heaven. As I prayerfully attended to this joy, I pondered what I was being invited to "catch" in my ongoing formation as a guide and follower of Jesus.

The doorway of my believing and active imagination opened, and I saw before me a formal invitation card, which read, *"Julian Jacobson is invited to a Master Class on Human Formation."* Intrigued by the reference to "human formation," I was keen to attend, for I had witnessed Gideon's "spiritual formation." The card instructed me to attend to a significant moment in Gideon's formation that morning.

I saw Jesus beckoning to Gideon at the side of the river. Two weeks earlier, Jesus had beckoned to Gideon when he was conscious of the little boy's fears of loneliness and abandonment. Gideon's image of the wounded child, the child's poignant question, "Where were you?" and the picture of the child asleep on Jesus' breast spoke to me of the intimacy between creature and Creator. Gideon's hesitancy to join Jesus in that previous session revealed not so much a crisis of belief as a fear of relational commitment, a fear that clearly plagued other significant relationships. As I revisited this in the context of my "master class," I could see that his breaking through this fear was a deeply human response that would have significant ramifications for his relationship with God and others.

I could see that Gideon's deepening intimacy with Jesus had offered him a safe relational space in which he could extend understanding and compassion to a core part of his wounded childhood. Up until that point, he had felt totally alone with the pain of his abandonment—so much so that he had sought to lock away the experience deep within himself. In his awakening, Gideon had experienced the touch of the One who knew abandonment, and so had discovered that he was not alone—and had never been alone. The One who shared most deeply in his experience had always been with him, actively seeking him, waiting for that little gap to open up when he might notice him. As a seeker, Gideon had discovered that he was being sought—and had always been sought. Jesus had been waiting to beckon him home!

---

4. Neh 8:10.

As I meditated on this epiphany, I thought of the waiting father in the parable of the prodigal son, opening myself to all I could recall and savor of Gideon's account of his interactions with Jesus. I remembered that when Jesus beckoned to Gideon, there was complete freedom—no judgment, no hint of pressure or coercion, just patient waiting for Gideon's response. As I recalled Gideon's interior freedom, I experienced it myself and reflected on how true human growth, formation, and transformation occur in the context of relationships that offer such complete freedom.

As I experienced this interior freedom, I felt the steadying hand of the master teacher prompting me to bring my attention to how these movements had gradually formed between Gideon's spirit and the spirit of Jesus. Attuning the eyes of my heart to Gideon as he was gently drawn back into that place of relational intimacy with Jesus, I glimpsed a tiny thread moving from the heart of Gideon to the heart of Jesus, and then from the heart of Jesus back to the heart of Gideon.

Pondering this gentle interplay, I was struck by the interactive and reciprocal nature of this sacred encounter, which provided the relational space for Gideon's initiation into the fuller life of the kingdom. Jesus had beckoned Gideon into this relationship with the welcome and joy of the father at the return of his prodigal son.[5]

At the beginning of the session, Gideon had expressed confusion about the meaning of "initiation," but rather than someone explaining it to him, Jesus had embodied it for him through the story of his baptism, inviting Gideon to become an onlooker and then a participant. Jesus himself had become the *bridge* for Gideon to cross into an intimate and participatory relationship with the triune God, a relationship central to his formation as a human person.

I recalled my anticipation and hope as Gideon stepped forward, then the inner jolt when he experienced anew the trauma of being drowned in the dark and sinister waters of the cavern. Facing these waters in the company of Jesus and John, he had not had to bear this burden alone. In Gideon's death and burial in those waters, he joined in the death and burial of the One beckoning him into relationship. And when he broke through the surface, he rose from death to new life, from one allegiance to another, from the kingdom of this world to the kingdom of God.

In the prayer "in earth, as in heaven," I could see that as the kingdom comes, we descend into the deepest wounds of our human experience and

---

5. Luke 15:20-24.

PART III: RESTORATION

die to all that has estranged, entangled, and entrapped us. In that moment, the heavens open and the Spirit of God descends,[6] and we glimpse the new life of Jesus' kingdom and the heart of the One who is continually creating and transforming us. Gideon had stood on the threshold of this abundant life—freed from what had held him captive, initiated into the life of the kingdom—ready to offer his fealty to the King, who was also his friend and his brother.

The joy, amazement, and gratitude that had accompanied me into my time of prayer and reflection now gave me wings, and from this higher vantage point, I could see Gideon wading through the Red Sea to be freed by God from the captivity of his Egypt experience.[7] He was stepping away from the dominant cultural imagination that had entrapped his identity and vocation, surrounded by a great community of witnesses who had also experienced God's liberating deliverance.

I knew that there would be much more for me to catch as I journeyed with Gideon—and other pilgrims—as I prayerfully witnessed them becoming active participants in the kingdom of God, stepping into a narrative that stretched right back to the beginning of human existence.

I ended my reflection with the words "Your kingdom come. Your will be done, on earth as it is in heaven."[8] I had indeed glimpsed the glory of the Lord.

---

6. Matt 3:16 –17.
7. Exod 20:2.
8. Matt 6:10 NRSV.

11

Recovering Lost Identity

During the week, Gideon phoned to ask if Judith could come for part of the next session. Given his despondent tone, I intuited that things between them were shaky. I recalled Gideon speaking of his difficulty committing to a long-term relationship. I reflected on the constraints that Gideon had been relinquishing and the new life that was emerging for him, aware that his relationship with Judith might suffer because of the changes he was making in his life. We agreed that Judith should come about twenty minutes into the session to give Gideon an opportunity to talk over their relationship.

When Gideon came for his session, he slumped in the chair across from me and said, "Judith says she needs space."

"What happens for you when Judith says she needs space?" I inquired.

"I don't need space—I need Judith."

The weighty silence that followed clicked by like a metronome at its slowest speed. "Whenever she talks about needing space, I fill up with fear ... it grips me right here." He placed his hand over his heart.

"What do you notice as you feel that fear grip you?" I asked.

Gideon dropped his head, and I saw the metronome's pendulum swinging from new freedoms to old fears.

"I know the name for this fear is abandonment, but I also know that I need Judith."

"You can name the fear 'abandonment.' Can you stay with the 'need' for Judith?"

"I feel like Judith is my other half, my soul mate, but as I say that, I can hear the neediness in it."

"Neediness," I repeated.

"As if I'm afraid I won't survive without her, that I won't be a whole person."

There was a knock at the door, and though I could see that Gideon was nervous, he rose to greet Judith.

I welcomed Judith and thanked her for coming. As Gideon introduced us, I could see in her eyes and gestures that she was there out of kindness, rather than any hope in her relationship with Gideon.

When Judith looked at me, I nodded, and she took a deep breath, then spoke words that she had clearly rehearsed. "I know my stepping back has hurt you, Gideon, but you have become possessive and I feel smothered. You have this glorified image of me, yet are so negative about yourself. Love is not a possession but an embrace in which people grow and discover how desirable they are. I can't make you accept yourself as loved and desirable." She sobbed and reached for tissues.

I marveled at her insightfulness as I grieved that Gideon's discovery of his belovedness in the sight of the Lord had come too late for her.

In the silence that followed, Judith regained her composure, then said gently, "I know I sound harsh, and I regret that, because I care about you. But I know that our relationship is not good for either of us."

When it was clear that she was finished, Gideon said, "Your honesty has helped me stop pitying myself long enough to realize what a gift our relationship has been. You have spoken from a deep place of truth, and I admit that when I came here today, I'd hoped to plead with you for one more chance, with Julian here to tell you how much I've changed." He wiped tears from his face, then said, "But to plead with you wouldn't honor what you have just said."

"Thank you for letting me speak so honestly." She glanced at me, then said, "Now I think you should have time to continue without me here." As we stood, Judith shook my hand and thanked me, then kissed Gideon lightly on the cheek before leaving.

As Gideon and I resumed our seats, he lapsed into a long period of silence, sighing and shifting in his chair. I could see that Judith's words had touched a painful nerve.

"Though I did not want to admit it, I could see that coming," Gideon said at last. "I was consumed with Judith and had become so possessive and smothering." He paused, then asked, "Has the smothering I so hated in my mother become part of me?"

Gideon looked up at me for an answer, so I reflected back, "You are recognizing important truths in what Judith has said."

"I suppose my secret hope was that Judith would see how far I'd come along the path of healing and restoration, and I was seeking her approval more than the One inviting me into deeper life."

"As you realize that you may have looked more to Judith than to the One who was inviting you into deeper life, what begins to happen for you?"

"I'm back trying to win approval in the hope that lifelong intimacy might follow."

"What do you notice about that place of trying to win approval?"

"I'm drawn back into that pattern of seeking intimate relationships so desperately that I lose my focus on the One who wants to fill my inner void. I can see now how I might have lost myself in my relationship with Judith—and smothered her in the process."

"Can you say more about losing yourself in your relationship with Judith?"

"I have been puzzling over what Judith said about it being beyond her capacity to help me know myself as loved and desirable. I think she could see that I was trying to find my identity in the context of our relationship. I was looking to her to mirror back my sense of self, but I was too blind to see it."

"What were you too blind to see?"

"That I had been trying to find my identity from people and projects—my old pattern."

"As you name this 'old pattern,' what do you notice next?" I asked.

"If I look back on the 'crisis' that brought me to your door many weeks ago, I see that a profound truth was unearthed within me when I engaged with the baptism of Jesus and heard him named as God's beloved son. I resonated strongly with that moment, as I recognized Christ's identity as one who was filled by God's Spirit and named as his son."

"As you touch that inner truth when you recognized Jesus' true identity, what begins to happen?"

"The invitation before me now is to establish my identity upon a firm foundation. It was beyond Judith, my parents, or my work to provide that foundation."

"They could not provide that foundation."

PART III: RESTORATION

"Only Jesus, who knew himself as a beloved son, could restore my identity as a beloved child of God. Of course Judith alone couldn't help me see myself as loved and desirable. I was adoring her without growing in love myself. But the encounter I had with Jesus and the little boy has helped me know myself as loved and desirable." Gideon paused, then cried out, "But it all came too late for Judith!"

12

In God Alone My Soul Finds Rest

Walking in solidarity with Gideon through the truth and the pain of his relationship with Judith had roused within me the uneasy feeling that something had been broken that could never be mended. Though I might have been stirred to shed tears for Gideon and Judith, the tears I shed during my evening time of prayer and reflection were for the old loss that had broken my own heart many years before. As I reflected on what had transpired in my morning session with Gideon, I saw the half-shape of Gideon with Judith as the lost puzzle piece that would complete the picture.

As I brought my prayerful attention to this incomplete figure of Gideon, I remembered how Judith had spoken of love not being one-sided adoration but an embrace in which people grow and discover how desirable they are. The conviction undergirding her words conveyed that they had arisen from careful reflection on her own experience. Her words had stirred Gideon to recognize that he was seeking his identity externally, from people and projects, rather than through a deepening relationship with God.

As I continued to reflect on how this wisdom had emerged for both Gideon and Judith, the half-shape figure of Gideon began to fade, and I saw a figure of Gideon joined by a second figure, who offered him a cloak. I realized that the second figure was Jesus, clothing Gideon in the cloak of Trinitarian love.

As I watched this scene unfold, I became prayerfully attentive to the grief of Gideon's and Judith's loss as well as my own loss of a loved one some years past, and I acknowledged this awakening as a prompting of the

Spirit. I remembered my own journey through the dark tomb of aloneness and how it had become a womb for new life and growth as grief gradually befriended me and the One who knew the brokenness of my heart invited me to place my feet in his trustworthy footprints. This part of my story was a deep part of myself, and the Spirit was moving me to place it in the service of Gideon by drawing me back into those painful memories, that I might move forward in deeper sensitivity.

I prayed that my guiding work might reflect and embody the *way* of Jesus as he humbled and emptied himself for service.[1] Pondering Christ's vulnerability in this act of humility, I offered my experiences to God, trusting the Spirit to bear my prayerful reflections to the places within Gideon where such sensitivity was needed.

This morning I had been struck by the depth of Judith's intuition and how what had come from her heart had opened Gideon to painful revelations about his relationships. What had happened between Gideon and Judith had occurred within an active "community of presence" that included me as well as the Spirit. As an active player in this community of presence, Gideon had been able to acknowledge his poverty of spirit, grieve his losses, and willingly come to a place of meekness before God. In the previous session, Jesus had called Gideon to participate actively in his life and purposes. Today, Jesus was drawing him toward relational wholeness by clothing him with love.

As I came to the end of my prayer and reflection, I recalled the sorrow around Judith's departure. But by the creative and transformative presence of the Spirit, Gideon and I had journeyed over the chasm of grief for lost love to fellowship with the triune God, where love is restored and we find rest for our souls.

---

1. Phil 2:7.

13

Raised to Life

At the beginning of our next session, Gideon settled into the chair across from me and asked, "When you were young, do you remember creeping up behind friends, putting your hands over their eyes and saying, 'Guess who?' Well, something crept up on me this week, but I feel like my eyes are still covered and I can only guess what it is all about."

Gideon paused, then continued. "It was my turn to lead Bible study, and the passage was the restoring of Jairus' daughter and the healing of the hemorrhaging woman.[1] The richness of these stories drew me in and the preparation went well, but as I was leading, I felt intense sorrow as we read of the little girl's restoration to life and the woman's healing. Some of the group must have noticed my distress, because they asked what had happened. I told them I was affected by the story, but I knew something more was happening."

"Afterwards, one of the older members, Bob, asked if I would lead the same study for the men's recovery group, because they were such great stories for men. He explained that stories that have the capacity to bring deep spiritual transformation to men will invariably contain feminine elements."

"Later that evening, as I held my responses to these stories along with Bob's comment in prayer, I saw myself during my last year of primary school and I also saw my mother. I felt stirred to bring this to our session to give it more attention."

"As you recall these events, what do you notice is before you now?"

---

1. Luke 8:40–56.

"I see the distraught figure of Jairus, setting aside his legal and religious work, hurrying to search out the healer for the sake of his sick daughter." Gideon shaded his eyes with his hands. "Jairus' urgent search is quickening my heart rate, and I feel the same sorrow I experienced with my Bible study group. I am falling with Jairus at the healer's feet as Jairus begs him to come to his house, where his daughter is dying. As the eyes of the healer fall on me, I hear myself say, 'It's my twelve-year-old as well, but I am not sure if he is lost or dying.'"

"As this query about 'your twelve-year-old' arises, what does the healer do next?"

"He takes my hands away from my eyes," Gideon replied, removing his hands and looking up at me.

"What about the 'twelve-year-old' do you see?" I asked.

"I see a boy coming out from the shadows. He's rubbing his eyes and shading them from the bright sun." Gideon paused. "I hardly recognize him, but I know that he is me."

"What happens for you as this boy emerges from the dark and you hardly recognize him?"

Gideon became fidgety, and I felt a sharp pain in my heart as I intuited that Gideon was on the threshold of a painful memory.

After a long silence, Gideon said, "At first, I felt I was back in the crisis that brought me to you. Fear argued that it was not safe to open the door in front of me. And when I opened it, these negative emotions and jumbled memories hit me, knocking me to the ground. I'm not sure if I'm dead or alive." Gideon exhaled, then dropped his head.

"Even though fear told you that it was not safe to open the door, you opened it and were hit by negative emotions and jumbled memories. Now you are lying on the ground, unsure if you are alive or dead."

Gideon slowly raised his head. "I feel as if life is being drawn out of me."

"Can you watch over yourself as you lie on the ground?" I asked.

Gideon lowered his head and closed his eyes, remaining silent for several minutes. Then he said, "As I watched over the figure, I began to pray over him, and slowly the emotions and memories settled. I felt frustrated because the most prominent emotion was 'abandonment,' and I thought I had already dealt with that. Then I resolved to protect my heart from any more pain, but as I say that, I am feeling considerable pain, even though I still don't know if the figure of me is alive."

"As you feel that pain and the uncertainty of whether the figure is alive, what do you notice next?"

"The twelve-year-old is kneeling next to the adult, trying to rouse him."

"Can you understand what the boy is saying?"

"He is saying that he is the one who has been lost and left for dead."

"What happens to you as you hear him say that 'he is the one who has been lost and left for dead'?"

"How could a twelve-year-old be left for dead?"

"What would it be like to ask him?"

"I would like to, but the strangest thought has just come, and I'm hesitant to say it because it's so confusing."

"Can you stay with the thought and the confusion?"

"It's as if part of me is dead to something, lost and dead to a memory."

I felt a sharp pain as I heard the words "lost and dead," but trusted Gideon to Christ's mercy during the silence that followed, intuiting that he was on the threshold of a traumatic memory.

"What do you notice in front of you?" I asked gently.

"The figure of the adult is sitting up next to the boy, and the boy is trying to get him up so he can walk."

"Can you look around with them and see what they see?"

"Jairus is still on his knees before Jesus, so the boy and adult move to sit with them."

In the silence that followed, the sharp pain intensified, along with a current of hope.

"In the presence of Jesus and Jairus, time is standing still. Even though I know Jairus is anxious to go to his daughter, his story pauses, and there is space for the story of the boy and me to unfold."

Over the next ten minutes, the memory that had been lost and left for dead came alive before Gideon.

"During my last year of primary school, my father remarried. He and his new wife went to Spain for six months so he could meet her extended family. I moved to my mother's house, leaving my friends and changing schools. After the marriage, my mother became increasingly withdrawn, then stopped leaving her bedroom. For two months, I cared for her, but then she refused to open her door. I rang my grandmother, who was living interstate in an aged care home. She became very distressed, for she knew it was impossible to come, but she told me to ring the local general practitioner and police. The doctor arranged to admit my mother to a psychiatric hospital, and the police took me to a group home to await a foster family."

As Gideon remembered his time waiting in the group home, he saw an image of the boy being tumbled around inside a clothes dryer. His distress intensified when he realized that the boy had no way of reaching the controls.

"He desperately needs someone to help him!" he exclaimed. With tears filling his eyes, he continued. "I couldn't understand why my father didn't come straight home from Spain. I still can't. I know I wrote to him and told him that the foster parents were kind and that I was all right, but I wasn't. Maybe I was just trying to pretend I was brave to gain his approval. A father should know when a child desperately needs him. I felt angry when he came to collect me from the foster home three months later. I wanted to say, 'You are three months too late!' but I couldn't because I needed his love more than ever."

"What happens when you notice that the boy is in desperate need of help and his father does not come to care for him?"

"I am back with Jairus and the healer, who are walking towards Jairus' house and his dying daughter. I feel Jairus' urgency, because we are hindered by the crowd. The healer has stopped and is asking, 'Who touched me?' Amidst the confusion, I see the woman with the hemorrhage touching the healer's cloak. But it is very strange, because I recognize the woman as my mother. I can't look at her!" Gideon cried, covering his face with his arms. "The pain on her face is piercing my heart."

"The pain on her face is piercing your heart," I repeated.

"The pain of what is happening to her as they take her away in the ambulance, her pain for me, and her pain at being separated from me."

"The pain of what is happening for her, her pain for you, and her pain at being separated from you," I reflected back, encouraging Gideon to stay with the pain.

"As they took her away, I felt so guilty for failing her—but I was also relieved that someone else was going to help her." He sobbed. "During the three months I was at the foster home and she was in the hospital, I only saw my mother once. I let her down when she was so sick."

After the highly charged silence that followed, Gideon whispered, "My mother is pointing to the healer and back at herself. Now Jesus is saying to my mother the words he said to the bleeding woman: 'Daughter, your faith has made you well; go in peace.' When he spoke those words, the guilt I've been carrying was swept away by peace that my mother is well!" Gideon's face shone with joy rather than being darkened with grief.

"The crowd is saying that Jairus' daughter has died, yet the healer urges us to continue, even as the crowd ridicules him. But I can't see my boy anymore! Now the healer is taking the dead girl by the hand and saying, 'Child, get up!' He looks at me and I hear his command echo: 'Child, get up!' I see my boy now—he is with Jairus' daughter!"

Gideon retreated into silence, his face still shining with joy. After several minutes, he opened his eyes. "I am remembering how Jesus turned water into wine, but the way I've structured my life can't hold the new wine that has flowed today."

I nodded, deeply enriched by Gideon's insight.

"I am also wondering about Jairus and how his life might have unfolded. But as I think of him, he asks, 'What will you do from this point on?' Will I rebuild my protective walls and draw indelible lines around my relationships? Or will I seek a 'new wineskin' in which a twelve-year-old boy can roam freely and not feel lost and left for dead?"

In the peaceful silence that concluded our session, I held Gideon's questions as prayers before the healer, filled with wonder and gratitude for God's presence in our midst.

14

Establishing the Work of Our Hands

"Will I rebuild my protective walls? Or will I seek a new wineskin?" Gideon's questions echoed in my mind as I opened my evening time of prayer and reflection with lines from Psalm 90.[1]

> Let the beauty of the LORD my God be upon me.
> Establish Thou the work of my hands;
> establish Thou the work of my hands.

We are never told how Jairus lived after his encounter with Jesus, and I marveled at how this story from scripture had awakened Gideon to deeper questions about his own life. In reading and studying scripture, he had invited the gospel story to "read" him, mirroring back his own story as the Holy Spirit enlivened the text and drew him into the transformative encounter with Jairus, the unnamed woman, and Jesus. Like Jairus and the unnamed woman, Gideon had experienced a miracle when the "left for dead" twelve-year-old part of the story had been resurrected. Through the movement of the Spirit, he had realized that this transformation could impact the way he lived his life.

As a privileged witness to Gideon's encounter with the Living Word, I prayerfully reflected on Gideon's questions: "Will I rebuild my protective walls? Or will I seek a new wineskin?" These questions led me to reflect on my own journey. Will I draw closer to the points of intersection between

---

1. Ps 90:17 KJV.

these stories of Jairus, the woman, Gideon, and Jesus? Will I continue to trust the intersection of gospel stories with pilgrims' lives and my own life?

I reflected on how the gospel story had compelled Gideon through his emotional connection with Jairus' sense of urgency. When Jairus begged Jesus to come because his twelve-year-old daughter was dying, a door opened within Gideon, and he was invited to enter the story with the unexpected thought, "I think it's my twelve-year old as well." In the presence of Jesus, these two stories intersected, and a "left for dead" memory was brought from darkness into light.

When Gideon and the boy had knelt with Jairus before Jesus, Gideon had noticed that time was standing still, opening a space in the story for Christ's healing and love to enfold him. I wondered if this could be an invitation for me to become more sensitive to such enfolding in a pilgrim's story.

I could see in hindsight that the gospel story, which had been brought to life by the presence of the Spirit, had faded into the background when Gideon had encountered the "left for dead" twelve-year-old boy. Yet the story from scripture continued to hang as a backdrop of hope when Gideon connected with his lost memory. I recalled the poignant moment when Gideon had seen the adult figure sitting up next to the boy, uncertain where they were to go. Though it would have been easy to forget Jairus and Jesus at this point as I focused on the challenging task of walking with Gideon through his painful memory, I remembered wondering if Jairus and Jesus were still there. I had known I needed to trust the gospel story to do its work, and so had asked, "As they look around, what or whom do they see?"

In reflecting on this risk of forgetting to trust and follow the gospel story, I was reminded of Jesus' words to Thomas: "Have you believed because you have seen me? Blessed are those who have not seen and yet have come to believe."[2] Again, I heard the echo of Gideon's questions before me: *Will I?* Will I walk through excruciating places of pain with pilgrims and still believe? *Will I?*

When the boy's story appeared to have come to an end, and Gideon had experienced an image of him being tumbled around in a clothes dryer, he had experienced distress. This distress intensified when he spoke of his father not coming back from Spain to care for him. But then Gideon reported that he was back with Jairus and Jesus. As I gave thanks for the Spirit's work in guiding Gideon back into the gospel story in the midst of

---

2. John 20:29 NRSV.

his desperation, I heard Jesus' words, "Come to me, all you that are weary and are carrying heavy burdens, and I will give you rest,"[3] as a silent refrain.

As Gideon had dwelled with the image of himself and his twelve-year-old boy resting next to Jairus in the presence of Jesus, another figure had emerged: the woman with the hemorrhage. In her face, Gideon saw his mother and connected with her pain, which pierced his heart.

Through this experience, the Spirit had led Gideon to reclaim a part of his story that was vital to his healing and restoration. Poised in the background, the Living Word—as embodied in the gospel account of Jesus—says to the woman, "Daughter, your faith has made you well; go in peace." In these loving words, the voice of Jesus leapt over the bounds of space and time to assure Gideon that his mother would be well. I was privileged to hear Gideon's account with my own ears, but will I stand with those "who have not seen and yet have come to believe?"[4] *Will I?*

I returned to Gideon's insight regarding the questions he had raised about Jairus after his daughter's resurrection. Though we never hear the rest of Jairus' story, nor that of his resurrected daughter, the story echoes with the possibility that there was more life to come for them. In the same way, will I trust with Gideon that there is more life for him and for his resurrected twelve-year-old boy? In following the footsteps of the One who has healed and transformed us all, will I trust that there is new life for my own story?

In closing my time of prayer and reflection, I gave thanks for the unfailing love of the Lord, which had fallen upon me and Gideon through the Living Word. "Lord, I will. May your beauty fall upon me and establish the work of my hands."

---

3. Matt 11:28–30 NRSV.
4. John 20:29 NRSV.

15

Defensive Batting

During our next session, Gideon told me about his father's love of cricket and his many cricket trophies. He added that he had not been able to live up to his father's expectation of him as a cricket player. "Though I was passable with a cricket bat, I never took to the game," he explained. "I know that was a real disappointment to him." Gideon paused, then continued. "When Dad would come to watch a match, I was so excited, but in his presence, I would poke at the ball and fumble it in the field. When practicing at the nets with my friends, I did fine, but with Dad around, my batting was defensive."

I waited in the silence that followed, holding Gideon's discouragement in the face of his father's disappointment. "Dad's mother, my Nana, would come to stay with us for three or four weeks at a time through my early teen years. I felt very close to her and loved those visits. Like my Granny, she lived interstate and was not able to come when my mother was in hospital, as she had to care for my Pa after he was disabled by a stroke. But when my Pa died shortly after my father returned from Spain, she was able to visit us."

"She would come to my cricket matches and watch my dad and I practice while she worked in the garden in the front yard. One time, after my dad had left in frustration at my poor batting, I threw down my bat and flopped beside her as she tucked plants into pots. Without looking up from her work, Nana said, 'I wonder if you bat that way because you are cross that your mum and dad are not together.'"

"Her words touched something deep inside me. My cricket improved after that conversation, even in the presence of my father. And Dad seemed to take more care in managing his own disappointment when I batted poorly or fumbled the ball."

Gideon sighed and looked at me. Sensing that the monologue had exhausted him, I reflected, "You say your father changed a little and your cricket improved, even in his presence." Gideon nodded. "I wonder if you can imagine what was happening for your father."

Gideon shifted in his chair, then said, "I have been so preoccupied with what happened between me and Mum that I haven't thought much about Dad." He paused and closed his eyes. "I feel a little for him as I remember how he changed."

"Can you spend time with this 'feeling a little for him' and notice what comes?"

Gideon's eyes grew distant and reflective. "My dad had a stroke recently. I think I want to see him and talk about what has been happening for him." After a brief pause, he looked at me and said, "I wonder how I might approach that?"

"Can you imagine yourself in a conversation with your dad?"

He settled into his chair and closed his eyes. "I see myself as an adolescent boy, decked out in cricket gear, setting aside my bat."

"What do you notice as you put your bat aside?" I asked.

"I need to become less defensive in my dad's presence. I also need to stop blaming him for all that happened to me. I need to forgive him for not immediately coming back from Spain to care for me. He has been different since his stroke—more vulnerable, searching for ways to connect with me."

Gideon grew silent and reflective. After several minutes, I asked, "What have you been noticing?"

"Most of the change will need to happen within me," he replied. "When I realized that Dad didn't know how to respond to the little boy, something shifted for me. I am sure he did not know what to do with me, especially with all the tension he was experiencing with my mother and the challenges of his second marriage. As I notice what is happening for him, I am discovering more compassion and love—the same love and compassion that I felt Jesus extending to the lost twelve-year-old boy. I trust this love and believe it is wide enough to stretch across what has always felt like an impassable divide between my dad and me. There's still so much we need to learn about each other."

Gideon stood. "I am glad we talked about my dad today. I feel prepared to go visit with him." Though our conversation had been short, there was much for Gideon to pray about and act upon in his relationship with his father.

16

Beyond the Father Wound

As I came to my time of prayer and reflection, I reflected on how Gideon's formation through relationships had been a consistent theme: his relationship with Jesus, the relational insights that had come during Judith's visit, and his relationship with his parents. Rather than being at center stage, Gideon's parents appeared in the wings from time to time. Gideon's mother had emerged as he re-experienced the trauma of the twelve-year-old boy, appearing through the woman with the hemorrhage. Through the manifest presence of Jesus, Gideon had experienced healing in this relationship as he came to deeper clarity about what had happened with his mother and felt stirred to feel compassion for her.

Gideon's father had appeared through his cricket memory. When the doorway opened to attend to the relationship with his father, Gideon was more ready than he would have been several months ago, indicating that his relational formation had been building through the intimacy and freedom he was experiencing with Jesus.

In traditional psychology, a therapist would use the label "father wound" to describe the relationship between Gideon and his father. Although these labels can be useful, applying them does not build the bridge that will straddle the divide between fathers and sons. Some years earlier, there had been a movement encouraging young men to confront their fathers about the wounding they had experienced. I had been critical of this movement, because I felt it encouraged sons to project what they did not like (or could not acknowledge) about themselves onto their fathers. Such victimization erodes one's ongoing formation by encasing the wound and writing in stone the life trajectories that have been driven by it, rather than seeing the sacred possibilities of the wounding as a doorway into the presence of the Holy, into greater life and deeper and more fulfilling relationships, including relationship with God.

As I prayerfully reflected on my journey with Gideon, I was drawn to the response of the disabled man lying at the pool of Bethsaida when Jesus asks, "Do you want to be made well?"[1] The man responds by placing the blame for his incapacity on others: "Sir, I have no one to put me into the pool when the water is stirred up; and while I am making my way, someone else steps down ahead of me." Jesus calls to the "Yes!" buried beneath the man's victimhood with the instruction, "Stand up, take your mat and walk." With this invitation, he extends a bridge to the new and more abundant life that is waiting for the man on the other side of blame.

Even though Gideon had built up patterns of resistance to protect his heart from the pain of abandonment, I was encouraged by the growth I had witnessed as he imaginatively interacted with his parents. By the gentle stirring of the Spirit and Gideon's growing intimacy with Jesus, Gideon had been able to face the truth about his wounding and journey away from blame toward understanding and compassion. I gave thanks to the Spirit for guiding Gideon away from blame and over the bridge of this deeper "yes" as he followed the *way* of Jesus.

I had walked across this bridge also as I had sought to reach out to my own father, realizing as I did that he was reaching out to me. Through my adolescent years, he was often away interstate or overseas with his business. At each special event at my school, I would build up hope that I might see my father's face in the crowd, then steel myself against the probability that he would not appear. I remember walking past my friends as they climbed into their father's cars to be driven home. As I turned the next corner, out of their view and down the hill to the railway station, I would kick at the gravel, scuffing my shoes. I could understand that he was a busy man, but he was stoic as well. Yet change had come in his retirement, when my mother had a stroke and lost much of her speech. His stoicism dissolved as he cared for her and, little by little, we began to have conversations.

My father and I found a bridge, and as I walked across it, away from blame and resentment, I discovered the tragedies that were part of his story and realized why he had needed to defend his heart through stoicism and busyness. When, in my late fifties, I entered further into the interior places

1. John 5:2–9.

that harbored the residue of a "father wound" and opened it to the light of Christ, a doorway opened that drew me closer to my aging father and into deeper intimacy with my Heavenly Father. My father wound had become a "sacred wound."

As I closed my time of prayer and reflection, my heart filled with gratitude and my mind flooded with sweet memories.

17

Returning from Exile

Gideon began our next session by describing the discouragement he was encountering amidst his positive change and growth. "I have been feeling new passion, fervor and enthusiasm for my team at work and my faith community. I am still grieving my loss of Judith, but I have made good progress in understanding why things went the direction they did. And yet ... something still stands in the way of me going deeper with my father. I have been dwelling on a snide remark he made at my award ceremony. It's like a tape that keeps playing over and over."

I offered back to Gideon the contrast he had made, holding the positive change and growth in my left hand and the haunting tape in my right hand. I then reduced that to: "Growth and yet the old tapes!" Gideon moved his gaze from my left to my right hand and back again, mirroring my hand actions as he inwardly held the contrast.

"Now that is strange," he said. "The word that comes to me is 'exile.'" He looked puzzled.

"There is your very evident growth, there are still the old tapes, and now the word that comes is 'exile.' Can you stay with 'exile'?"

"My recent changes are establishing new patterns, but my old patterns of exile still remain and are blurring the boundaries of those changes."

"Can you stay with this 'blurring'?"

"The blurring is rather dark grey," Gideon said.

"As you stay with that dark grey, what do you notice about it?"

"An adult figure has just emerged from the dark grey mist. He is shadowy, like a silhouette of a person."

"As you bring your attention to the silhouette of this person emerging from the dark grey mist, what do you notice?"

"He is very active," Gideon replied. "As I focus on his movement, the word *fervor* comes back to me."

"What happens next?"

"There is a boy emerging to his right."

"As the boy emerges, what draws your attention?"

"He is much clearer than the silhouette. The boy is me, and he is very busy, but I can't see what he is doing."

"You can see that the boy is you and that he is very busy. Can you watch over him and observe what is happening for him on the inside?"

"He tried so hard!" Gideon cried out. "Why couldn't his father see that?" he sobbed. "But that little boy just kept on trying and hoping. The closer I come to him, the more familiar that desperation for love and approval is. It's raw and painful in the boy. It was there for the adolescent. And though I have tried many ways to cover it up, it is there for the adult as well. I've been so preoccupied with my projects, hoping for something that my father and mother weren't able to give."

"Hoping for something that your father and mother weren't able to give," I repeated.

Gideon shifted his position in the chair. "You remember, Julian, in one of our earlier sessions, you invited me to look into my mother's face?"

I nodded.

"I am being drawn back to that same place," he continued, "but the boy is older." He paused. "Actually, both the boy and adult me are looking at my mother, who seems very preoccupied. Something is taking all of her attention."

"As you and the little boy notice that your mother is very preoccupied, what happens for the little boy?"

"He thought she was ignoring and rejecting him. But together, we can see that she was just withdrawing inside herself and was not able to reach out to the boy because of her pain. I wonder if I am being invited to see more."

After a long pause, Gideon continued. "My mother smothered the boy sometimes—he hated that! But we see that she was smothering him because of her unresolved emotional needs, almost as if she were trying to live out some of her unlived life through him." He paused. "I started today talking about the 'tapes' of my father's remark. My mother's response at the award night was to take on my achievement as her own."

"When you acknowledge this as the 'adult Gideon,' what happens to the boy?"

"He is more relaxed and seems relieved that he hasn't done something to make his mother swing between rejection and smothering. He is showing concern for her."

"As you see this shift in the boy's attitude toward his mother, what is happening for you?"

"The boy is transparent, and I can see a dark thick thread tangled up inside him, like a thick root wrapped around the region of his heart."

"As you notice the shift in the boy's attitude, you see something like a dark root tangled around his heart."

"The word that comes as I look at the dark root is *resentment*."

"As you discover that the dark root that entangles his heart is resentment, what do you notice next?"

"It is so familiar," he said with a deep sigh. "But when I see it and name it as 'resentment,' the little boy becomes agitated again, and I can feel that root moving around my heart." He massaged the region around his heart with his right hand. "And there is a bitter taste in my mouth."

"You can feel the root of resentment moving around your heart," I said, mirroring Gideon by rubbing my own heart, "and there is a bitter taste in your mouth."

"Yes," he replied, "and as I attend to these things, I see my father. With my father, the resentment is about his demands and his inability to give me his approval. When I look at the root of resentment in the boy, I see two thin threads, but they join and thicken."

"As you notice the two threads of resentment join and thicken, what do you notice next?"

"I have been aware of resentment toward my parents, but I never realized how huge that root was, nor how fully it was trying to strangle my heart. I want to get it off, but I know I cannot move that root on my own!"

"What happens as you realize that you can't move the root on your own?"

"I am remembering how John the Baptist sent my burdens down the river. I need forgiveness for the bitterness and release from the root. That is what I am asking for now."

In the silence that followed, I knew that Gideon was inwardly confessing this deep root of bitterness in his life and seeking the forgiveness of Christ. When I sensed that he was finished, I spoke words of forgiveness and release in Jesus' name. Though our session had begun with discouragement, it had become a place of transformation, guiding Gideon into profound relief and new freedom.

18

It Is Written

In my prayerful reflection that evening, my attention returned to the inner struggle I had witnessed occurring in Gideon. I had seen how Gideon had stored up debt in his soul, entangling his heart with a dark root of bitter resentment that he was powerless to extract. In this place of powerlessness, I had sensed the presence of Jesus through the Spirit as he invited Gideon to unlock new freedom in his life by confessing his resentment and forgiving his parents. As I had sensed the presence of Jesus in the room, I had felt stirred to speak words of forgiveness in Jesus' name, knowing that without that forgiveness, Gideon's inner "debt" of bitterness would stand in the way of growing intimacy with his true guide.

During our session, I had been witnessing a life-and-death struggle. In my imagination as I reflected and prayed, I saw Jesus during his fasting for forty days and nights in the wilderness.[1] I remembered Jesus' three temptations: to turn bread into stones, to throw himself down from the pinnacle of the temple, and to gain all the kingdoms of the world in exchange for worshiping the tempter. In these temptations, Jesus had wrestled with his human needs for security and sustenance, affection and esteem, and power and control. When I placed Gideon's temptation to hold onto his bitterness alongside these temptations, I realized how Gideon's "temptation" had also been rooted in unmet needs, particularly for affection and esteem.

Jesus had relied on scripture ("it is written . . .") to unmask and name his own temptations. When tempted with the human need for security and

---

1. Matt 4:1–11 NRSV; Mark 1:12–13; Luke 4:1–13.

sustenance, Christ had responded with what was written: "One does not live by bread alone, but by every word that comes from the mouth of God." When tempted with the human need for esteem, Christ had responded with what was written: "Do not put the Lord your God to the test." When tested with the human need for power and control, Christ had responded with what was written: "Worship the Lord your God, and serve only him."[2]

Though Satan's temptations were strategic and cunning, the true guide's responses were sharp as a sword, as if Jesus were holding the palm of his hand firmly against the tempter, saying, "Go no further." This encouraged me to name my basic temptations and find clear and unequivocal responses to them. At the same time, I had a fleeting image of Gideon holding the palm of his hand against the temptation of bitterness, saying, "It is written: Honor your father and your mother!"

As I held this image, I cherished the fulfillment of Jesus' sojourn in the wilderness. The gospel account states, "Then the devil left him, and suddenly angels came and waited on him."[3] I recalled how Gideon had remembered more of Jesus' love and compassion in our previous session. In today's session, Gideon had received the gifts of forgiveness and freedom. This had been like the sudden appearance of angels, waiting on Gideon and bringing him the gifts of love, compassion, forgiveness, and freedom. Neither Gideon nor I would ever be left to struggle alone against our temptations!

I closed my prayer time by expressing my desire to continue to grow in intimacy with my Father God and in devotion to my true guide.

---

2. Matt 4:3–10 NRSV.
3. Matt 4:11 NRSV.

Part IV:
Experiencing Grace

19

Wild, Extravagant, and Unexpected Grace

At our next session, Gideon opened with, "This past week, I landed head first in the prodigal's pigpen. I have never thought of myself as a prodigal, but I certainly know the pigpen!"

"You are saying you know the pigpen," I reflected, anticipating that this parable was leading Gideon toward deeper insights.

"Remember when I was struggling to describe how I was feeling totally overwhelmed? I've realized that my pigpen is that dark underground mine, that deep cavern, my ocean grave."

"As you acknowledge the underground mine, the cavern, and your ocean grave as your 'pigpen,' what happens for you?"

"I feel like the prodigal coming to his senses!"[1]

"Can you describe coming to your senses?"

"After the prodigal was embraced by his father, he could still look back and remember wading through the pigpen. I look back and see myself wading against a dark torrent of negative emotions and fears, like an addict keeping to my habit, even as I become more deeply mired. The prodigal had to starve to come to his senses. I had to drown!"

In the heavy silence that followed, I wondered inwardly if Gideon had been drawn back to that "life-death" struggle.

"The parable had to shock us!" Gideon said, looking up at me.

I asked, "What happens for you as you understand that the parable had to shock you?"

1. Luke 15:17.

"Like the prodigal, I couldn't be lifted out of my pigpen. I had to awaken to its grotesqueness."

"Can you stay with, 'awaken to its grotesqueness'?"

"Just when I saw my most dejected and grotesque self I met the Father! The One who gave me the freedom to squander all he had given me and then patiently awaited my return, the One who ran to greet me and welcome me home."

"As you encounter the Father at your most dejected point, what do you notice?"

"I am encountering a wild, extravagant, and unexpected grace—a response I neither deserve nor anticipated."

"On the one hand, this was a response you did not deserve or anticipate," I said, holding up my left hand. "On the other hand, you encounter a wild, extravagant, and unexpected grace," I said, holding up my right hand. "What happens as you look from one hand to the other?" I asked.

Gideon glanced back and forth between my hands. "If I go to the not deserving and not anticipating side," he began, "I am drawn back to the son asking for his share of the inheritance and the father dividing his estate. Though that seems distant from my experience, I'm wondering how I might have done that."

"What begins to draw your attention?"

"I see myself on the observation deck of the tower with my boss telling me the world is my oyster. But now, this moment of crowning glory is all distorted. Instead of looking down at the expansive view of the city below, I'm looking down the mouth of this water slide that terrified me as a child. I'm on the edge of a nightmare, without space to breathe—yet there is something light about it all. I feel like laughing at myself!"

"As this scene of 'crowning glory' becomes distorted, but with a lighter edge, what happens next?"

"My boss seems amused at my response to his words, and he gives me a friendly shove into the water slide. I don't resist him, but just watch myself falling."

"You don't resist, but watch yourself falling."

"Now I've landed on my hands and knees on the tile floor of the tower foyer. I am looking up at the figure of the cleaner, who is accusing me of messing up 'her' tiles. And the whole thing that horrified me before is now mildly amusing."

"Mildly amusing."

"Like Alice in Wonderland," Gideon responded. "It's like being flipped over to get an upside-down perspective." He paused. "But I'm not being turned upside down, am I? I'm being flipped the right way up!"

"From that 'flipped' perspective, what do you notice about the scene in front of you?"

"Until the cleaner spoke of those tiles as 'hers,' I had considered the whole tower mine—even an extension of myself. I had taken her claim to the tiles personally, but now I feel indifferent."

"Indifferent," I repeated.

"The cleaner helped me detach my identity from the tower. The tower was always indifferent to me, and now I can be indifferent to the tower."

Intuiting that the prodigal son had more to mirror back to Gideon, I asked, "In this place of detachment from the tower and new perspective, what do you notice about how you might have 'divided' the father's inheritance?"

Gideon remained silent for several minutes, then said, "I've been living the one life that has been given to me. Over the past months, I've been awakening to the knowledge that what is most true within me is to be found in my relationship with God. So what have I been doing with my divine, God-given inheritance?"

Gideon looked troubled, and I could intuit that he had encountered more shadows of himself. "I don't believe I was wrong to put my creativity into project managing that tower, but I divided my inheritance when I became preoccupied with it, and it became my 'crowning glory' alone. I was holding onto God, calling myself a Christian for my own glory, rather than living as a reflection of His glory."

"Can you stay with the dividing of the divine inheritance?"

"My 'far country' was my total absorption in my work life. And while the prodigal attached himself to a reckless and self-serving lifestyle, I attached myself to the self-serving values of corporate life. I put everything into building my own tower. And while I was doing that, I convinced myself that I was living as a good Christian man."

I could see that Gideon was puzzled as he reflected on the contradiction before him. "When I revisit the tower's observation deck, where I stood with my boss, I see Jesus being taken up a high mountain to view all the kingdoms of the world. Satan tells Jesus that everything can be his if he falls down and worships him. Jesus sends Satan away with a real sting, quoting from scripture: 'Worship the Lord your God, and serve only him.'"[2]

---

2. Matt 4:8–10 NRSV.

PART IV: EXPERIENCING GRACE

"What happens as you bring together your boss's words to you on the tower, Satan's words to Jesus on the high mountain, and Jesus' clear and definite response?" I asked.

"My boss and I are both caught up in something seductive and sinister. Building the tower wasn't evil, but we colluded with darkness—and gave up our souls—when we took the glory for the tower ourselves."

"You colluded with darkness and gave up your soul."

"To bring that project to fruition, I had to make so many complex decisions and overcome so many obstacles. To conquer those obstacles, I had to transcend myself."

"To transcend yourself," I repeated.

"As I hear the word *transcend*, I realize that it has a spiritual edge to it—and that is part of what is so exciting about creative work. Rather than using the gifts God gave me for his glory, I took my divine inheritance and became addicted to it, pushing myself harder and faster, which led me to the edge of total collapse."

"Your divine inheritance brought you to the edge of collapse," I repeated.

"When I divided my divine inheritance, I gave 'it' my primary allegiance, rather than the One who gifted it to me. 'Tower worship' overshadowed 'God worship,' and self-interest and corporate materialism usurped the Sermon on the Mount. Through the parable of the prodigal son, this prodigal"—Gideon pointed to himself—"is being invited to return from that 'far country,' where I created my own idols, and go back home to my primary allegiance with God, my father."

"Can you say a little more about the 'far country' you are returning from?"

"The far country must be about distance—not geographically, but the way I became distant from my soul. Judith helped me see how distant I had become from those I loved. I'm sure my aggressive and single-minded seeking out of materials for the tower project numbed me to true stewardship of God's created world. In my preoccupied state, I became oblivious to most things around me—and so I became distant from God."

"Where is Jesus inviting you to go as you return from that far country of 'distance'?"

"I'm right back with my prodigal mate. He is sitting in his pigpen and I'm sitting among the ruins of my tower. When I named the tower as my idol, it must have imploded!"

"As you sit in the ruins of the tower, what begins to happen for you?"

"The prodigal is inviting me to go home with him, but it will take a long time because we've wandered so far." Gideon fell silent, and his face grew weary, as if he were trudging along on a slow, arduous journey. Then his countenance lit up as he exclaimed, "We know how this parable unfolds! The father is running toward us, welcoming us home. I didn't think it would have anything to do with me! Even though I climbed to the top of my tower and it fell into ruin, the father is welcoming me home with love, mercy and wild, extravagant, and unexpected grace!"

"And as you encounter that wild, extravagant, and unexpected grace, what do you notice?"

"The word *restoration* has come to me. I'm being welcomed home and restored."

In the long silence that followed, I observed the expression of wonder on Gideon's face and felt that wonder bloom in my own heart.

"The word *restoration* has flowed out of me and is touching the things around me—my drafting table, covered with dust, which I am wiping off now. I have just found a drawing of the tower in perspective—an invitation to see all of my work in perspective. And as I say that, I can see the tower—completely intact, lifted from the ruins. I see my colleagues and boss, wishing me well—not there to puff up my identity, but just there as themselves. And now there is my father." Gideon paused and bit his lip as he fought back tears. "There is my father just being my father."

Gideon reached for a tissue and blew his nose. "In the restoration I'm being offered, I can see all that was so distorted from a new perspective. It was not wasted—it is a part of my history. Somehow what I might have achieved and thought to be my crowning glory now has meaning as work for the glory of God."

"As you attend to this experience of restoration, what do you notice?"

"For the first time . . . I feel real joy, and I don't know whether to laugh or cry. But here it is, and I believe it has come to stay."

"On the wings of wild, extravagant, and unexpected grace," I said, reflecting back his words.

"On the wings of wild, extravagant, and unexpected grace—joyous grace!"

On those high notes of joy and grace, our session came to an end.

20

Enlivening the Imagination

The compelling interplay I had witnessed between Jesus' parable and Gideon's story reverberated in my mind for the remainder of the day. As I entered my evening time of prayer, I reflected on this "watershed moment" for Gideon. As the mystery of our session lifted its veil, I realized that the session had also been a watershed for me as a guide.

As I had witnessed the interchange between Gideon and this timeless parable of a father and his two sons, I had received the gift of watching the Spirit of God reveal to Gideon a "parallel parable" through his particular story, guiding him to see how he had divided his divine inheritance so that he could be liberated from his own "pigpen" and receive the gift of God's wild, extravagant, unexpected, and joyous grace. Now, a doorway was opening through which I was being invited to walk—not only as a witness but also as an active participant.

Like Gideon, I had always loved this parable and had often taught about its capacity to turn us upside down and engage us in the alternative imagination of the redeeming, restorative, and reconciling possibilities of God's kingdom. But Gideon had been willing to be fully engaged by the parable—and so by the spirit of Jesus—and this had grounded the parable in human experience for me. Over the past months, I had sought to stand in solidarity with Gideon in the pain of his human experience, and this morning I had received the gift of standing beside him as the shalom of God's kingdom broke within him.

As I drew near to this place of shalom, I became aware of an intense longing and felt stirred to draw even closer to the Spirit's transforming grace. Could I encounter God's wild, extravagant, unexpected, and joyous grace as Gideon had? Was Jesus inviting me to be destabilized by this parable as well?

As I meditated on these questions, I lifted my gaze to Sieger Köder's painting of the prodigal son, which was hanging on my study wall. Inwardly, I felt the Spirit prompting, "You have been looking at this painting for more than three years. Now it is time to step across the threshold and enter the doorway that is opening for you!"

© Sieger Köder, *Der verlorene Sohn* [The Prodigal Son].

I placed myself in the space occupied by the prodigal son in the painting. I imagined the father's face fitting against my head and neck as he embraced me. I felt his large, gentle hands resting on my shoulders. The father's right eye was buried in the nape of my neck, but I could see his half-closed left eye, and it was completely focused on me, his child, who had been lost but now was found, who had been dead to him but was now alive. In the comfort of this father's embrace, I closed my eyes and rested.

When I returned my gaze to the painting, I noticed the elder brother leaning up against the doorpost, hidden from his father's view, watching his father embrace his younger brother. In a stark and disturbing counterpoint to the warmth and trust of the father, Köder conveyed the elder brother's jealousy, anger, and judgment in his depiction of this rigid and secretive figure. As I studied the elder brother, I sensed the residue of my self-righteous judgments, and I struggled to distance myself from his grotesque figure. But my eyes kept returning to his hidden, dark form, and I realized that like the elder brother, I saw myself as undeserving of grace.

My left hand, like the elder brother's, was covering the tight fist I was making with my right hand, as if to hide what I had just discovered. When it occurred to me that the elder brother might be hiding away a stone, I opened my fist and relaxed my hands as a question formed within me. "What if the elder brother and I, rather than the father, had been meeting our prodigal brother?"

I knew that in the prodigal's day, his family and villagers would have practiced *kezazah*—a permanent rejection of one who squandered family money among foreigners. By the practice of *kezazah*, the father could have said, "This one who was once son and brother and who was dead to us should remain thus!" What were the stones in my hand? How did I practice *kezazah* in my context, society, and culture? In what situations did I choose to blame rather than extend compassion? When did my society scapegoat those living on the edge—as I stood by and watched in silence? I thought of the incarceration of desperate asylum seekers illegally crossing national borders. By standing with the elder brother holding the stone, I was being invited to unmask the subtle societal and cultural pressures that limited the measure of my compassion. Where did I need to extend mercy rather than doling out what I felt the "prodigals" I met deserved?

Standing with Gideon this morning had brought me close to his nearly unwitting collusion with corporate and material culture. Now I was being invited to reflect on my own attachments, allegiances, and addictions—grotesque distortions that invert God's shalom. Like Gideon, I am in need of redemption, restoration, and reconciliation.

In the past, I have tried to squeeze into the space against the doorpost that Köder places between the father and his elder son. But I am conscious of my longing to step beyond that threshold, away from the disgruntled posture of being undeserving of grace. When I complain, condemn, or criticize, I am holding onto that doorpost with the elder brother. In this state of "undeserving" anxiety and fear, I sulk on the edge of rage when I should be running to a celebration.

ENLIVENING THE IMAGINATION

I lean toward the father. Part of me has always wished that he would be closer to the middle ground—a bit less wild, more domesticated, less of that tough love and more room for sentimentality. Yet as I become a participant in Gideon's dramatic engagement with Jesus' parable, I realize that the middle ground is not where the father is! The father flaunts protocol, sacrificing his dignity, reputation, and status. At the first sighting of his son in the distance, he wildly outruns *kezazah* in order to declare that this son who was lost and dead is now very alive to him. In this extravagant, risky, and unexpected reinstatement of his wayward son to full and honored status in both family and village life, the father becomes *prodigal* in his actions. With such love and mercy, there is no middle ground.

That middle ground squeezed between the elder son and the father, with its subtle masking of uneasiness about grace, leaves me feeling unworthy and fretful over the slow and often piecemeal signs of restoration in my person and in the lives of pilgrims whom I seek to guide. If I take a gigantic leap from the middle ground to the far edge I land in the place where risk meets sacrifice. This is where the kingdom of God reigns over the earth—for the redemption, restoration, and reconciliation of prodigal pilgrims. This reigning God does not protect his heart from our reactions, rejections, and treachery but becomes *prodigal* for us, his prodigal people!

Would I, like Gideon, live on the edge of this wild, extravagant, and unexpected grace? Would I step away from the middle ground and live on the edge of this kingdom, as imaginatively portrayed in Jesus' parable? I knew I didn't want to camp out in the middle ground of a limited imagination. I wanted to take that leap into a redemptive, restorative, and reconciling imagination, expectant of the shalom of God within and around me. I prayed for God to "reclothe" both Gideon and me in this new kingdom life.

I closed my time of reflection and prayer with deep gratitude. As I rested in this space of gratitude, I remembered the psychiatrist whom I had consulted about Gideon's circumstances. She had spoken to me of taking Gideon's "deeper pulse"—and today, in cooperation with the Spirit and through his parable, I could feel that heartbeat emerging.

21

Wooed by Joy

"So much happened the last time we met," Gideon said at the beginning of our next session, "and much has continued to bubble within me these past two weeks."

"Could you say a little more about that bubbling?" I asked.

"You know how a great play or movie can keep you in its grip long after it has ended, often both disturbing and surprising you? It's been like that, except that I haven't been observing the drama—I've been part of it."

"What has disturbed and surprised you as you have participated in this drama?" I asked.

"I was disturbed and surprised by how readily I fit with the words of the father in the parable of the prodigal son: that I was dead and now am alive. By acknowledging that I was dead, something has come alive within me. I want to welcome this new life, yet I have been frustrated because I can't identify what I'm trying to welcome."

"Something is coming alive within you, but you are frustrated because you can't name it," I reflected back.

"I wonder if I'm being awakened to this new life, but it isn't something I can work out in my mind. Maybe I just have to wait for it to be revealed. I know that God is working in me, and so I am trying to acknowledge and welcome God."

"Can you say a little more about acknowledging and welcoming God?" I asked.

"The word *released* comes to mind. When God broke open the box of my cramped imagination, he offered me a glimpse of his wild, extravagant welcome. I am trying to invite God to guide me into that wide and spacious reality."

"What did you notice as that box of your imagination was broken?"

"I wanted to welcome God—the God of Jesus—with both hands. I had to know more about this God! So I read John's Gospel, Paul's letters, Isaiah, and then, while reading an old poetry book, I found 'God's Grandeur,' by Gerard Manley Hopkins."

"What happened to you in this search?"

"I was bursting with excitement, praise, and wonderment. I just kept saying, 'Yes, Yes, Yes!' But there were also moments when I felt overwhelmed and afraid."

"You felt excitement, praise, and wonderment, but at times overwhelmed and afraid," I reflected.

"When I realized that I couldn't 'box' God in with descriptive words or metaphors, I was exhilarated. I know that God is releasing something in me—I can feel it happening!—but I can't get a full handle on it, and that's scary. What's happening to me, Julian? What is being released?"

"If you allow those two questions to sit before you, without looking for a direct answer, what happens?" I asked.

"Over the past two days, I have been remembering my dreams and have wanted to speak with you about them."

"So the questions become, 'What's been happening to me in my dreams? What might my dreams indicate about what is being released in me?'"

"That's it!"

"Would you like to take a moment to find the place where you are being guided?"

Gideon sank further back in the chair, closed his eyes, and dropped his head. In the long silence that followed, I prayed to be faithful in holding the space for the Spirit to awaken Gideon to his dreams. As this period of stillness expanded, I anticipated the in-breaking of the kingdom of God.

"I thought I might be taken to a particular dream," Gideon said at last. "But I've been taken to a woman who has appeared in many of my dreams. As I asked myself why this woman was familiar"—he shifted uneasily in his chair—"I have been catapulted back into some of my darkest nightmares."

"Asking yourself how you know the woman in your dreams has put you back in your darkest nightmares," I responded. "What do you notice about the place into which you have been catapulted?"

"It's that dark and sinister cavern again," Gideon shuddered, grasping the sides of the chair. "But I'm reluctant to go back there." He tightened his jaw. "But if that's where I'm guided, then so be it."

"Back to the dark cavern," I echoed.

"My nightmares often thrust me into this cavern, and then the critical, angry voices from this cavern started spilling over into my waking life. After my split with Judith, this woman started appearing in my nightmares, and we would explore the cavern together, but there was always this distance between us. I could never get close enough to see her face. Even though I didn't like being in the cavern, her presence was reassuring. But in the nightmares, as we walked through the cavern, I would realize that we were walking on top of a frozen lake. Then I would see the woman fall through a hole in the ice, but she was always too far away for me to prevent her from falling or to pull her out. Then I would wake in a state of panic." Gideon pressed his hands against his eyes.

"Then one evening, during a long, restless night, I reached her in my nightmare, but her hand slipped out of mine and she fell through the ice, as always. When I woke, I felt completely surrounded by darkness, as if I had been dropped into a deep abyss. I was so terrified that I started to cry in desperation, 'Help me! Help me!'" Gideon's body convulsed, and several moments passed before he could continue.

"Somehow I fell asleep and slipped back into the nightmare, back to that moment where I felt her hand slip through my fingers. I heard her cry, 'Help me! Help me!' as she fell through the hole in the ice. But I was able to plunge my hands through the hole, grab her wrists and pull her to safety on top of the ice." Gideon slumped back in his chair. "I overslept the next morning and woke to the warmth of the sun streaming through my bedroom window. As I stretched and opened my eyes, I felt alive and free, and I kept hearing the echo from that parable: 'once was dead and now is alive.'"

"You felt alive and free, as if what once had been dead was now alive."

"A few nights ago, I met this woman I'd saved from the ice in a lush green meadow outside the entrance to the cavern, where there was a flowing stream. She invited me to dance, but I resisted, though I felt envious of her freedom and grace. As I watched her dance, I lay in the soft grass, and I felt overwhelmed by intense emotions—first tears, then joy. Even though I know it was only a dream, I can still feel those emotions." Gideon smiled, his eyes still closed, as if basking in the richness of those emotions.

"Then last night, when the woman extended her hand and invited me to dance, I was eager to follow her. She led me to the top of a slope in the meadow, where the wildflowers were in full bloom. At the top of the rise, she rolled down the slope through the grass until she came to rest on the level ground. She sprang to her feet, tossed back her hair and laughed, though I also noticed tears in her eyes. I followed her, and though I haven't ever really rolled down a grassy slope before, in my dream it was exhilarating!" He laughed, and I smiled at the image of this young man rolling down a grassy slope like a child.

"I was so absorbed in rolling down the grassy slope," he continued, "that I didn't notice the woman moving away. I searched until I found her sitting on a log by the stream with her head in her hands, weeping. Not wanting to startle her, I waded through the stream so that she would hear me coming. When she realized I was there, she parted the canopy of her long hair with her fingers and smiled at me, though her tears continued to flow." Gideon paused, as if looking intently at the woman from his dream. "I think she was inviting me into freedom and joy, but she was also revealing her sorrow, showing me that she, too, has been wounded."

After waiting with Gideon through a long period of silence, I asked, "What happens for you as you notice the woman's joy and sorrow and realize that, like you, she has been wounded?"

"My empathy has brought me closer to her. Because she has let me see her tears, I have been more comfortable with my own weeping—and my tears no longer feel so desperate, but sorrowful. Even when I am weeping, I am thinking of the Beatitudes and how mourning and grieving follow on from acknowledging our poverty of spirit—and that leads me to joy and gratitude!"

Gideon looked at me, his eyes wide open in surprise. "As you come to that place of joy and gratitude," I said, "I wonder what it would be like to glance over everything that has emerged today from your dreams and nightmares. Where are they inviting you?"

Gideon closed his eyes and shifted his hands on his lap. Finally he said, "There is a whole neglected part of myself—a frozen part that is beginning to thaw. Even sorrow has a place in my life, and that has come as gift."

After a long and peaceful silence, Gideon said, "You know, Julian, in our last session, I was offered the gift of joy. Today, I am being invited to feel deeply, to know both sorrow and joy. So the joy I feel now is deeper. My striving before was to know about God with my mind, but now I want to know the God of Jesus with my whole person—my heart, soul, and strength." Gideon paused. "Many months ago I came to know 'grief,' but I did not know until I met this woman, 'Joy,' in my dreams that they were so closely related."

Gideon drew a deep breath, then concluded, "I think I need to go and find a grassy slope to roll down!"

22

Treasures in Jars of Clay

Throughout the day, as I reflected on Gideon's journey, I heard the words, "surprised by joy," the title of a book by C. S. Lewis,[1] in which he mapped his search for joy through the territory of grief. As I entered the solitude of my reflection and prayer, these apt words knocked again at the edge of my consciousness.

During today's session, Gideon had experienced a joy that could both embrace his nightmares—the full range of his emotions, including his pain and grief—and also invite him to play, laugh, and weep freely and openly. In coming to the end of himself, Gideon had been awakened to this surprise of joy as the full texture of his human experience had been willingly embraced by God.

As I prayerfully walked through the morning's session, I, too, was awakened to the surprise of joy that does not shun terror, death, or grief. When I ingested into my own body the bread and wine, the body and blood of Christ each Sunday during communion, I was tasting of his sacrificial joining and transfiguring of joy and pain, terror and freedom, life and death. As this "upside-down" kingdom expanded in my own life, so did my sensitivity to the manifestation of these movements from life to death to greater life in the midst of each pilgrim's experience. This "kingdom imagination" lens enlightened my heart so that I could see what was being stirred to the surface of Gideon's life by the Holy Spirit. These "life-death" struggles of our spirit do not take place on neutral ground but are active tensions—tugs of war—between what is "life-giving" and what is "death-dealing."

1. Lewis, *Surprised by Joy*.

PART IV: EXPERIENCING GRACE

I had witnessed much life-death struggle in Gideon's story, including the initial thoughts of suicide that had prompted him to contact me. What grace that Gideon had not taken his own life but had awakened to the death-dealing aspects of his life—such as his compulsion to "divide his divine inheritance." By letting those death-dealing aspects of his life die, he had been awakened to deeper life and faith, and along that journey I had seen the alleviation of his distress, a drastic improvement in his self-esteem, a firming up of his identity, a greater willingness for self-discovery, along with many other positive "therapeutic" changes.

I had witnessed Gideon turn on a firm axis from self-reliance to a place of meekness and humility, open to his Creator-God as the central and sustaining reality in his life. My glimpses of transformation in Gideon came as reminders to continue to view life—my own life and the lives of pilgrims—through a kingdom lens as I attended to signs of shalom: contentment, wholeness, peace, justice, compassion, caring, sharing, laughter, joy, reconciliation, and a spirit of harmony with the inner self, others, the created world, and God. With this kingdom lens, I was being invited to look for more, hope for more, and pray for more along this path of transformation into the likeness of Christ.[2]

As my attention shifted between the therapeutic and kingdom imaginations, I recognized a significant difference between a professional "therapeutic alliance" (the relationship between the "expert" therapist and the "client," whom I refer to as "pilgrim") and humble cooperation with the guidance of the life-giving Spirit. If I was to reflect to Gideon the life-enhancing nature of Jesus, such a treasure would be contained in the unadorned clay pot of my person so that there would be no confusion about the source of this power. I knew that the extraordinary transforming power that had accompanied Gideon through pain, wounding, terror, loss, surrender, and dying belonged to God, not to me.[3]

Some months before, I had journeyed near Jesus through his passion during Holy Week. In my journey with Gideon, I could see how the life of Jesus—his suffering, death, resurrection, and ascension—was being released in Gideon's story, bearing with it signs of the shalom of God. With awe, I gave thanks that I had been able to be an unadorned clay pot, bearing witness to the love of Jesus for this pilgrim—and for me.

2. 2 Cor 3:18.
3. 2 Cor 4:7.

Part V: Participation

23

We Sat Down and Wept

Gideon began his next session by describing the practice of *lectio divina*, a prayerful reading of scripture that engages the heart as well as the mind by immersing one in the eternal life of God. He said that he began by reading a passage of scripture in a spirit of open attentiveness. Then he invited his mind to descend into his heart as he reflected on the words and phrases from the passage, noting what was drawing his attention. He then prayed in response to what the Spirit had prompted, seeking to remain attentive throughout the day to how the scripture might infuse and enliven his life. My prayer life had been richly formed by this practice, so I was pleased that Gideon had been introduced to it by a prayer group at his church.

In this prayerful and attentive manner, Gideon had read the parables in Matthew, where Jesus likens the kingdom of heaven to a treasure hidden in a field, a pearl of great price, and a householder bringing new and old things out of his storehouse.[1]

"What resonated," Gideon told me, "were the metaphors of the treasure and the pearl—it was as if I discovered them after they had been hidden within me for years. But I was puzzled about bringing the old and the new out of the storehouse. I felt prompted to look for the kingdom of heaven within and around me, so that the 'newness' of this kingdom vision might infuse and enliven whatever work was right before me each day. This filled

1. Matt 13:44–52.

me with passion and excitement! Then, as I prayed about how to do this, I felt stirred to reflect Jesus by leading my work team as a servant."

Gideon took a deep breath. "The day I prayed this, my team was presenting our tender, drawings, and model for a homeless shelter to the organization responsible for managing the shelter and the government officers involved with the funding. As we prepared for the presentation, I stepped back and let my colleagues take center stage. My boss, Malcolm, said, 'Even though I was disappointed that you passed up a big project for this shelter, you have the opportunity to do something impressive if they accept our tender.' With the servant thing still foremost in my mind, I replied, 'You know, Malcolm, there are some things far more important than all of this.' I had never seen tears in the eyes of this confident, self-made man; he was wiping them from his eyes as he said, 'I hope my own discovery is not too late.'"

"Later, as we were leaving, I noticed Malcolm hanging back, and I invited him for coffee. As we sat in a quiet corner of a cafe, he shared that his wife had been diagnosed with breast cancer. 'Marjorie seems to be handling the news better than me,' he confided. 'I know I need to be strong for her, but my whole world is falling apart.'"

"After we wept together, I asked if this might be his own discovery of what is more important."

Gideon paused to look at me. "I think you've taught me to be a more attentive listener, Julian, because suddenly he was talking about the harshness of his childhood. I've worked with Malcolm for years, but I've hardly known him before." Gideon paused, then said, "I guess I've been with 'me' all my life, but until recently I knew very little about myself."

In the silence that followed, I recalled the words of St. John of the Cross, who centuries earlier had said, "To come to the knowledge you have not you must go by a way in which you know not."[2] I felt certain that this was happening for Gideon.

When Gideon spoke again, he explained how whenever he prayed for Malcolm and Marjorie, he felt stirred to visit them. "But I had so much inner resistance to the thought of this visit that I asked for prayer from my faith community. My anxiety and resistance accompanied me right up to the door of their house, and I was tempted to turn my car around and head home. What could I say to a fifty-year-old woman who had just been diagnosed with cancer? Every line I rehearsed seemed inane. But when I

2. John of the Cross, *Selected Writings*, 78.

was standing on the porch, summoning the courage to press the bell, an inner voiced whispered, 'Gideon, you don't need set words.' When Marjorie answered the door, she took me in her arms and thanked me for coming." He shook his head and shrugged. "All I did was appear on their doorstep when they needed someone to listen and cry with them."

"You were resistant and anxious," I said. "You took the matter to prayer, then followed the encouragement to visit them and were welcomed into their lives as you listened to and cried with them."

"I don't think I have ever experienced such a deep encounter with people. When I have gathered with my faith community to pray, I've always felt marginal, but the encouragement that I didn't need set words was an important part of this visit, because it encouraged me to attend to Jesus as my servant guide, as if he were with me."

"As if he were with you," I echoed back. "Earlier you said you wanted to reflect the servanthood of your guide. As you reflect on your new approach with your colleagues and your visit with Malcolm and Marjorie, what do you notice happening?"

"As if I'm walking on the same road, but coming from a different location, without a roadmap. Even though the way ahead is unknown, I have this feeling that if I'm attentive to what is before me, I'll be able to rely on my inner compass."

"You will be able to rely on your inner compass," I reflected.

"During *lectio divina*, I felt prompted to look for the kingdom within and around me as I served my work team in imitation of Jesus, my servant guide. I can see now how Jesus faithfully offered me his guiding presence as I worked with my colleagues and talked with Malcolm."

"You can see how these parables about the kingdom accompanied you on that day."

Gideon nodded, then continued. "But that knowledge only comes in retrospect as I am prayerfully attentive to this new life of the kingdom."

"Do you remember saying that the parable about bringing out the old and the new from the storehouse was a bit of a puzzle?" I asked, sensing a prompt to return to this.

"If I were being brought out of a storehouse, there would be plenty of the old and a little of the new," Gideon responded with a grin. "There are still plenty of rough edges on me!"

After a long space of reflective silence, Gideon continued. "As I revisit my experiences from last week, two words are emerging: *spontaneity* and *sustainability*. After engaging with scripture prayerfully, I was able to step out in spontaneity with my work team and Malcolm. This way of prayerfully reading scripture will assure long-term sustainability. In looking for the new life of the kingdom, I realize that I have to put down deep roots into the old, so that my life and work will be grounded in wisdom and truth."

We concluded our session with a farewell, as Gideon had long known that we wouldn't meet again until I returned from a six-month sabbatical overseas.

24

A Road Less Traveled

Over a landscape pockmarked with craters of abandonment, relinquishment, and death, Divine Love had come to Gideon, guiding him through the valley of the shadow of death into new life. The stepping stones and bridges over this treacherous terrain had been fashioned from fragments of Jesus' broken body, transfiguring Gideon little by little so that he would become like love.[1] Gideon had responded to this free gift of love—this treasure, this pearl of great price—not by trying to preserve it as a trophy behind glass, but by freely giving it to others.

As I reflected on my morning session with Gideon during my evening prayer and reflection, I felt delight in recalling how Gideon had responded with servanthood to his work team and Malcolm and Marjorie. Enabled by a love and power greater than his own, he had made a deliberate choice to set out upon the "road less traveled."

To fully appreciate the significance of Gideon's choices and actions, I needed to remember the potential pitfalls, roadblocks, and diversions that are endemic to the intersection where transforming love touches our deepest wounds. For at this crossroads, I knew, many pilgrims had chosen to turn back or had become distracted by choosing other pathways. As I waited at this intersection, I discovered Jesus' parable of the sower.[2] "Let anyone with ears listen!"[3] I wanted to be "all ears" as I attended to Jesus' wistful pondering in this parable.

1. 2 Cor 3:18.
2. Matt 13:1–9.
3. Matt 13:9 NRSV.

PART V: PARTICIPATION

At this intersection, I could see a number of promising roads, and in my prayerful waiting, I could glimpse where they were going.

One of the roads gradually petered out—the road where pilgrims share their amazing experiences of transforming love with family and friends, "extroverting" these sacred moments rather than prayerfully pondering them in the presence of the Spirit so that they can penetrate deeper into their souls and bring new life. The precious seeds planted by Divine Love couldn't penetrate beneath the soil, and so they were eaten up by birds.

Down a brightly colored roadway, I saw pilgrims traveling swiftly and enthusiastically, fuelled by euphoria. Similar to "extreme sport" enthusiasts, these champions require constant applause and affirmation to continue along the journey, particularly when it gets arduous. Rather than carrying their transformed wounds, they try to flee from them. As the winding road of growing faith climbs into the rocky places, where true love begins to chafe and chasten, their euphoria quickly burns out. Rather than seeking to reflect back the love they have to others, these would-be champions look for affirmation, and when they fail to get it they search out other "highs."

Having experienced the new freedom of transforming love, some pilgrims choose to venture off alone in their quest of self-exploration and self-discovery, but this pathway can rise quickly to altitudes that starve pilgrims of oxygen. As the self is left alone to reflect on the self, these pilgrims breathe in their own stale air, losing sight of how deeper awakening can only come through relationship with God. If one remains on this road of self-preoccupation by seeking to hold onto the essence of Divine Love within oneself, one experiences the "high altitude sickness" of narcissism.

Pilgrims who continue to circle back to the site of their wounding, as a child's fingers will pick at a scab, close the window to further healing by lapsing into victimhood and claiming the company of fear, anxiety, self-righteousness, revenge, and distrust. Like the sower in Jesus' parable, I lamented those pilgrims who had followed the road of self-reliance, turning away from love rather than growing in compassion. Instead of receptivity, availability, and vulnerability, these pilgrims had reconstructed protective barriers around their hearts.

I recalled the following lines of William Blake's *Songs of Innocence*:

> And we are put on earth a little space,
> That we may learn to bear the beams of love.[4]

---

4. Blake, "The Little Black Boy," lines 13 and 14, in *Poems of William Blake*, 80.

To bear the beams of love would be to carry the scars and the piercings of our own transformed wounds, along with the heavy beams of Jesus' cross.

Gideon could bear those beams of love because he had set off with Christ, his treasure and pearl, in his heart. He had borrowed his true guide's coat of servanthood and had begun to participate in the life of the kingdom, acknowledging his need for the new while treading in the footsteps of those who had gone before him. He had chosen to invite the refreshing breeze of the Spirit to transform his wounds into "windows" of deep sensitivity and knowing in the service of other troubled pilgrims. Having taken none of the roads that circle back on themselves, he had avoided the dead ends of their entanglements and thorns. What he had been freely given, he continued to freely give.[5] His choice to move toward the extravagant dimensions of Christ's love had extended the boundaries of his soul and enlivened his spirit with glimpses of his Creator's grandeur and majesty. He had discovered that on this road, in the good company of Jesus and guided by the Spirit, he could tread lightly and not be burdened down.[6]

For several months, I had been preparing Gideon for my sabbatical absence, so I was full of gratitude as I reflected on how fully Gideon had embraced this road. As I came to the end of my time of prayer and reflection, I expressed my delight in the One who had guided us both, and I felt confident that Gideon would be companioned well during my absence. In preparation for my sabbatical, I prayed that like Gideon I would walk the "road less traveled" in the company of Divine Love.

---

5. Matt 10:8 NIV.
6. Matt 11:30.

25

Messengers from the Edge
Letters from Gideon

I spent the first month of my six-month sabbatical visiting the national parks of western North America, a tour of breathtaking vistas that culminated with the Canadian Rockies. For the second month, I entered prayerful solitude and silence at a retreat center nestled into a hillside on Bowen Island, one of the Gulf Islands off the coast of British Columbia, where my focus shifted from awe-inspiring external landscapes to hearing the whispers of God within the inner landscape of my soul. The rugged landscape enfolded me, and the interior silence was punctuated by morning and evening communal prayer and twice-weekly conversations with a wise spiritual guide. A verse from Job bound together the thunder of gigantic waterfalls and summer storms I had seen on my tour with the whispers of love I heard within the refuge of my retreat "cell": "Lo, these *are* the edges of His ways; but what a whisper of a word we hear of Him! And the thunder of His power who can understand?"[1]

This morning that same love accompanied me past the gateposts of the retreat center down to the island's harborside village. It was not time for me to leave the island, but it was the end of my silent retreat. For the next three months, I would focus on writing in a hermitage, rather than a cell, while joining other pilgrims at the main building for morning and evening prayer. I would also offer spiritual direction and lead an internship on spiritual companioning.

1. Job 26:14 NKJV.

My trip to the village was my first outing from the retreat center, and I was eager to gather supplies and check for mail at the village post office. With a large handful of mail, I walked from the post office to the village cafe, eager to sort through the letters while sipping a mid-morning coffee. When I saw three letters from Gideon, I set them aside and saved them to read over my lunch, as I wanted to take time first with letters from family and soak up long-awaited news of home. After watching the coming and going of ferries and the boats in the harbor tug at their anchors with the changing of the tide, I opened Gideon's first letter, which was also set on a harbor.

5th September

Dear Julian,

I trust that your invitation to receive letters from me will not intrude on your sabbatical. In one of our recent sessions, I mentioned how much I was enjoying the homeless shelter project. (We won the tender!) I didn't realize how close this project would bring me to the experience of homelessness, and at first I was uncomfortable meeting the people who would be living in the shelter. But playing pool and sharing meals with some of the men who are living in the rundown shelter that we'll be replacing has shown me how much I have to be grateful for. I also appreciate how they accept me for who I am—just a person, not an engineer.

Now that we've started construction, I realize that I have a passion for finding out what people who are living on the margins of society need, so I've accepted an invitation to present a paper at a conference on homeless housing. Because work has been so busy and stressful and I've been struggling to write the paper, I took a few hours off work yesterday to walk and pray by the harbor. As I approached a bench where I had often sat to pray and watch the boats riding at their anchors, I saw a man sleeping on the concrete, his head resting on a bag, his clothes damp from the rain the previous night.

The man's presence unsettled me, and I wondered why he had not used the old shelter, just a short walk away. Feeling relieved that I didn't recognize him and grateful that he was asleep, I kept walking. But as I tried to refocus on my conference paper, I felt ashamed that I had wanted to avoid him. When I came to the end of the path, I retraced my steps, and as I neared the harbor seat, I thought of veering away from him, but an inner niggling kept me on the pathway. As I approached the seat, he lifted his head and looked at me.

"Good day, mate," I called. "How are you going?"

"Going okay," he answered.

"Do you have anywhere to go?" I asked.

"I have everywhere to go," he said. "What about you?"

"I'm off to work, with a load to do." Before hurrying on my way, I asked, "Do you have any money, mate?"

His head dropped and he replied, "Nuh!"

"Do you have any food?" I asked.

Again, with his head down: "Nuh!"

"I can give you money to buy some food," I offered.

He raised his head and looked at me. "I don't accept money."

"I would be happy to shout you breakfast," I said.

"That'll make you late for work."

Here I had been writing about stigma in my conference paper, yet I was trying to avoid spending time with this man. "I'm . . . I'm taking a few hours off," I stammered. "What would you like?"

"Just a sandwich and some coffee," he replied.

"Wait about here, and I'll bring them back."

Back at home, as I made coffee and sandwiches, I resolved to sit with him while he ate.

When I handed the man the sandwiches and asked if I could join him, he gestured to the place beside him. For some time, we sat in silence.

Then the man said, "My father tells me you are the Good Samaritan."

"This morning I have been anything but the Good Samaritan," I said.

"This morning you have been the Good Samaritan," he insisted.

His words stirred something within me, and I began to weep. After a long space of silence, he began to teach me. I don't remember all of what he said, but he planted two seeds in me that I have not forgotten: "Jesus came into this world with nothing but his word," and "All we need in life is the love of God our Father." When he finished speaking, I introduced myself, and he told me his name was Adam. Then we shook hands, and he started to feed the birds the remaining crusts of his bread.

As I walked away, I thought about how Adam was living on the edge of society, yet he had taught me about hospitality; he was homeless, yet had everywhere to go; he was poor, yet rich with wisdom, which he had shared with me. As my thoughts drifted back to the conference paper, I realized with gratitude that Adam had just given me the theme for my paper.

If we were together, Julian, I imagine you asking, "As you have committed this story to paper, what do you notice happening within you?"

What strikes me is that I was full of contradiction, yet Adam was gracious and merciful to me. He had the capacity to hold my contradictions, and even though I stigmatized him, he beckoned to something more within me—and then offered me gifts.

As I stay with these gifts, I come back to his saying, "All we need in life is the love of God our Father." This man who has nothing, yet possesses everything, invited me into the presence of Jesus, where a contradictory and insensitive man was shown mercy and one who was "blinded" by relational wounding was shown that all he needed was the love of the Father. What a kingdom experience!

I trust that your sabbatical is going well and that you are in good health.

Your friend,
Gideon

~

30th September

Dear Julian,

I trust that the retreat center where you are staying for your sabbatical has good central heating, as winter will arrive soon. I am sure you are enjoying the autumn colors and carpets of leaves that you tread through on your daily walks on the island.

Our church has started a contemplative prayer group that is becoming a significant part of my week and is shaping my morning and evening daily prayer. It is a significant shift from the intensive and restorative work we did together—you, me, and the Spirit—and in the silence, I am beginning to rest in God and in who I am. When I cry, I am relieved to let the tears come without having to name or explore them.

In addition to relating to the homeless men around the shelter we are replacing, I am making friends with folks who are living in a supported living hostel near my home. Yesterday, after I came home from work, exhausted from the day's activities, I made a cup of tea, put my feet up, closed my eyes—and then the doorbell rang, a patterned and persistent buzzing that could only be Rob from the hostel. Annoyed that my solitude was being impinged upon, I muttered, "Go away, not now." But not wanting to pretend that I was not home, I opened the door to Rob's big, disarming smile.

"Got time for a chitchat?" he asked.

"Of course," I replied, intending to usher him into the kitchen for a quick glass of juice.

But then the light fixture in the hallway fascinated him, and he stopped to trace his finger along its textured glass. Each picture, vase, ornament, and book called for Rob's attention, and by the time he was seated at the kitchen table, he had to prompt me for the promised juice. With his "chitchat," Rob was showing me how to be more fully present.

As we drank glasses of juice, our conversation was slow and often stilted, with Rob repeating phrases, lapsing into long silences, or falling back on one of his stock questions, such as, "What do you think of the good ol' days?"

Despite my earlier resistance, I found comfort in Rob's face and the silence we shared at the table. Then Rob said, "Jesus follows me everywhere I go." He looked at me and asked, "Gideon, does Jesus follow you everywhere you go?"

A few minutes later, as I brushed tears from my eyes, Rob took his leave with a gracious bow, saying, "Thank you for the chitchat." We had spent no more than twenty minutes together, but the spirit of the One who followed him wherever he went remained in my house for the evening. The angle of the sun, now shining through the lead light, was casting patterns over the table, pictures, vases, and rugs.

As I watered the plants on my balcony, I reflected on how some weeks ago Rob had extended the peace of Christ to me after another long, stressful day at work. I had handled a meeting badly and had almost called Rob and some other friends from the shelter to cancel an invitation for tea, but had not wanted to disappoint them. Rob had been quiet that evening, but as I was leaving, he placed his hand on my shoulder and said, "You're a very good man, Gideon." Twice now, the peace and solitude I had so desperately sought on my own had come and found me through Rob!

May that same peace and solitude find you.

Your friend,
Gideon

20th October

Dear Julian,

When you first told me about your sabbatical, I confess that I was worried I wouldn't find someone to keep me on track. As you suggested, I am having a monthly session with a spiritual director, and that has been very helpful. My regular times of prayerful solitude, in which the Holy Spirit is my guide, continue to be significant, as I am learning how to sit freely in God's presence without evaluating my time of prayer. But what I never anticipated was that God's Spirit would send along other guides—first Adam, then Rob, and now I would like to tell you about Michael, another friend I have met from the hostel.

Michael, who might be referred to as intellectually disabled, says that he "was born to dance," and whenever he sees me, he invites me to his Wednesday night dance class. In spite of his persistence, it has taken weeks to break through my resistance. When I finally acquiesced, I was overwhelmed by the welcome of Michael's dancing friends and surprised by my relaxed enjoyment of the dancing.

Toward the end of the class, the facilitator welcomed each of us to move to the center of the circle to offer a solo dance for the group. The facilitator opened a safe space for everyone, recognizing their unique movements and affirming them when they were done. But nothing prepared me for Michael's dance, which was filled with grace and confidence and lacked self-consciousness. The obvious impairments associated with Michael's disability evaporated, and I could see clearly how he was born to dance, as the center of the circle became the holy ground where Michael found *home*. Years ago, he became isolated from his family, and his disability has relegated him to the edge of society, yet as he danced I could see the welcome of the father in the parable of the prodigal son. Though he lives at the edge of existence, he, too, has been swept up in that wild, extravagant grace and joy.

When I was welcomed into the center of the circle, I discovered inner freedom in my movements, even though I am very aware that I was *not* born to dance! I cherished the facilitator's affirmation as I returned to my chair, and I was moved when the man to my right leaned over, touched my arm, and slurred, "You're a great dancer."

It is a wonderful gift, Julian, to be able to write about this inner freedom to you, as you are so intimate with my story. I used to hold back in my dream encounters, and I finally see how much I was holding back myself. Michael and my other new friends don't hold back, and they are leading me to new edges—both without and within. When I move toward these friends, whose impairments and differences gain them undue attention, I am confronted with my own impairments. But when I am invited from the edge to the center, as I was in the dance class, I move beyond my impairments and wounding and so become less afraid of others who are wounded—like Adam, Rob, and Michael. And through their poverty of spirit, they have become my teachers. I have wondered for most of my life what I was born for, but Michael can tell me with confidence that he was "born to dance"—and he is helping me discover the purposes for which God created me.

Certainly you have not been replaced as a guide, Julian, but you have shown me how to receive the guidance of others who are living in step with the Spirit.

I trust that there are still some autumn colors and that you will survive the damp air and chilly rain of the coastal winter when it arrives.

Your friend,
Gideon

26

So Send I You!

I was fascinated by how Gideon was being wooed into the dance of those living on the edge of society. He was stepping away from the introspective solo of crisis and inner awakening to a new center, where his rhythm was being established by God's Spirit, and he was discovering new partners for a life-giving duet that was expanding his heart and the boundaries of his soul. Having been coaxed away from his inhibitions, resistances, and self-protective illusions of power and prestige, he was beginning to move more freely within himself and to embrace the "otherness" of friends such as Adam, Rob, and Michael.

With the letters spread out in front of me in the quiet of the hermitage later that evening, I brought Gideon's journey—and its impact on my own heart—into prayerful attentiveness before God. As I offered praise and gratitude to God for Gideon's shift in professional orientation and for his heart-stretching encounters with these new friends, the doorways of my memory were opened, and I felt stirred to celebrate both Gideon's journey and my own.

In the shift from designing high rises to designing homeless shelters, Gideon was following a descending pathway. Like Gideon, I had once been following an ascending academic pathway, but after a life crisis and transformative encounter with Jesus, I had followed a call to journey down the ladder. I, too, had experienced heart-stretching encounters with people on the edge, who revealed the protective barriers I had placed around my heart. Through their continued acceptance, I learned to bear both my open-heartedness and self-protectiveness before the living Christ as I humbly waited for the conflicting and contradictory sides of myself to be reconciled. In humbly recognizing my own contradictions, I knew that the spirit of Jesus had nurtured a space of peace for other pilgrims to journey toward reconciliation and wholeness.

"Peace be with you," I heard in my spirit. "As the Father has sent me, so I send you."[1] As Gideon faced fatigue and the need for solitude, Rob had come to reveal to him the limits of his hospitality and the residual hostility he employed to strengthen his personal boundaries. I remembered the jolt that I had experienced upon learning that Jesus did not seek to *protect* his heart but to *unify* it with the heart of his Father and so embrace the sufferings and pains of the world. How slow I had been to embrace the "otherness" of those who were different from me! Again, I heard the echo, "So send I you," reminding me that by bringing my heart into unity with his and welcoming Jesus in the multiplicity of his faces, I could continue to embrace the suffering and pain of diverse pilgrims.

Gideon's third letter about his experience with Michael's dance group touched a deep and tender place within me, a place of tears. The cry of the poor—in particular the anguish of friends living with mental illness—had emptied me of confidence in my professional methodologies and academic certainties. These cries had echoed over the ragged edges of my own interior poverty and had reverberated whenever I felt forsaken.

Whereas academic theory, with its concern for objectivity, had often directed my attention away from myself, my friends on the margins had broken through that screen of objectivity and guided me to my own poverty of spirit. Whereas I had once visited psychiatric hospitals to meet with professional colleagues, I now sat patiently listening to friends in waiting rooms and outdoor smoking areas. In their company, I learned to be silent, and I no longer feared what was dark and unknown.

"So I send you" I heard again as I reflected on how comfortable Jesus was among people of the edge. He would have been at home in Michael's dance group and had obviously been present there through the Spirit. Gideon had discovered that by moving away from the center of society toward people of the edge, who experience poverty daily, he came in touch with his own poverty of spirit. From that place, he was learning how to mourn his own losses as well as acknowledge his collusion with the power and violence that marginalized his new friends.

---

1. John 20:21 NRSV.

As Michael was welcomed to the middle of the circle for his solo, Gideon discovered a new center, where the edges of life and prayer become blurred. In the spaciousness of this center, power gives way to vulnerability, expertise surrenders to humility, and scarcity yields to abundance. In this circle, there is room for all—even for Jesus, who comes in the most transparent of guises. This was the spacious place I desired to open for pilgrims such as Gideon, and so I cried out, "Lord as you send me, put me closer to this place!"

The dance facilitator, who had invited Gideon and his companions to step onto holy ground, had also been sent by Jesus, just as the Father had sent him. Her grace-filled facilitation beautifully expressed cooperation rather than competition, and through her the Spirit reached out to embrace each participant. In this embrace, Michael knew that he was born to dance and that his dance would bring him home. In this circle, the anguish that is a constant experience for those living at the edge evaporates and is replaced by welcome into the heart and family of God. This exquisite cooperation with grace dignifies and ennobles each participant.

As I carefully folded each letter for safekeeping, I knew I was being prompted to celebrate how the experiences that had been awoken through Gideon's letters remained foundational to my growth as a person and as a guide in the *way* of Jesus. God seemed to be "sending" me to open a space for pilgrims that reflected the spaciousness of Jesus, as embodied in the dance facilitator. Like Michael, who had been born to dance, I was "born" to guide pilgrims, and my journey with pilgrims could become indistinguishable from my prayer, with a seamless transition from the companioning room to the temple of the Lord. This was something to celebrate!

Tomorrow I would write to Gideon.

27

From One Pilgrim to Another

Bowen Island
30th October

Dear Gideon,

I am writing to you from a little hermitage nestled in the woodlands near the retreat center that has been my home for the past month. This wonderful and challenging month of prayerful solitude followed on from four amazing weeks engaging with the spectacular scenery of the national parks of western North America.

In the last few days I have moved from my cell within the larger retreat house to a little log cabin, which is to be my hermitage for the next three months. It consists of one room plus a small bathroom. Within this space there is a large wooden table, which will double as a dining table and desk, two chairs, a kitchen counter with a gas stovetop, a small fridge, and a wood stove for heating. Part of my exercise, as autumn merges with winter, will be splitting logs to fuel this stove. My major exercise will be walking the heavily wooded and scenic pathways of this island.

Thank you for your three letters, which were held for me at the island post office during my month-long silent retreat. Over the last week, my prayer has centered on Jesus' Sermon on the Mount. As I sit at the table of my new abode with your letters spread out before me and my Bible opened to Matthew chapter 5, I experience Jesus' teaching coming alive in the rich encounters you describe. I sense his presence and his at-home-ness with you, Adam, Rob, and Michael. Through your thoughtfulness in sharing these experiences and your heart with me, I have felt included in that communion.

Just as I have traveled halfway across the world to this place of beauty, simplicity, solitude, and prayer, so you have journeyed deep within your heart to discover a unity and shared humanity with people who are located on the very edge of our society, who come as Christ to speak prophetically into our lives. Even as I write these words, I remember with great fondness and gratitude the Adams, Robs, and Michaels who spoke into my life—and those who still do.

Gideon, I would like to say a little about how Jesus' teaching comes alive for me through your letters. I am reminded of my need to come to terms with the ascendant aspects of my life and, in the spirit of the humility and meekness I find in Jesus' life and Beatitudes, to walk the pathway of descent that leads me to the less comfortable and secure edges of society and my own person. This emerged again for me during my retreat, and I see it happening in your life. I was deeply moved by your reference to Adam, Rob, and Michael as your guides. It is the guide who has no home but everywhere to go who reveals to us that our true home is found in our relationship with our Father-God and that God alone is enough. It is the guide who has little more to offer us than his own person who reveals to us the essence of true hospitality. It is the guide who knows that he was born to dance, and for whom dancing is prayer, who leads us from the edges of our estrangement to the true center, which is the source of our identity and vocation.

Isn't it amazing, Gideon, how our guides from the edge are freed to speak and act so prophetically, often turning us upside down? As I glance at the words "Blessed are the poor in spirit, for theirs is the kingdom of heaven,"[1] I remember how some of my guides—who knew what it was to be poor, even crushed in their spirits—mirrored back to me my basic illusions and vulnerabilities, my own poverty of spirit. When Jesus says, "Blessed are those who mourn, for they will be comforted,"[2] I think of my guides who experienced serious mental illness. Theirs is the mourning of fragile, anguished, and broken hearts, full of guilt and rejection, struggling against the odds to retain a sense of integrity, meaning, and purpose. Whenever I

---

1. Matt 5:3 NRSV.
2. Matt 5:4 NRSV.

stayed with the intensity of their mourning, the deep cries of their hearts awakened my fragile heart and brought to the surface things I needed to grieve. When I read, "Blessed are the meek, for they will inherit the earth,"[3] I have to ask, what better friends and guides to reveal meekness and humility than the Adams, Robs, and Michaels of this world?

Reading your letters alongside Jesus' Beatitudes brings so much to mind. Among these guides from the edge, I learned what it was to hunger and thirst for righteousness and justice, how my propensity to dominate stood in the way of my being merciful and working for peace, the impact of my having a conflicted and divided heart, along with what it meant to find solidarity with those who are marginalized, rejected, and even despised.

As these rich memories of my experience re-emerge, prompted by your letters and by Jesus' teaching, I am reminded that in all our rich diversity you, Adam, Rob, Michael, along with me and those of the edge who have guided me, are considered one body in Christ. We are members one of another.[4] Through the privilege I have had in journeying with you, as you came face to face with your poverty of spirit and came to acknowledge and graciously carry what has been most "real" in your life, I was able to review these aspects of my own experience. As you grieved your losses, I experienced a resonance within my soul, just as I did when the most painful parts of your lived experience received Christ's transforming touch. In our unity in Christ, we have both experienced being turned upside down—or rather, right way up—and reoriented to a stance of humility, meekness, and surrender. Thus to journey together becomes a living reminder of what it means to awaken to more abundant life and deeper faith.

Through your letters, I am a privileged witness to your deepening relationship with God. I see that through your growing intimacy with Christ, you have lifted your gaze and offered his welcome and embrace to those immediately around you, including those from the edge, whom you now call your guides. In the freedom that is being offered through their company, your capacity for mercy and reconciliation and your thirst for justice and righteousness will continue to grow—and a greater tolerance for criticism will be fostered within you.

So Gideon, you are in good company, and for that I am grateful. Over the next three months, as I continue my sabbatical on this beautiful island,

---

3. Matt 5:5 NRSV.
4. Rom 12:5.

you will remain in my prayers. Thank you again for the great encouragement I received from each of your letters.

Blessings to you in the name of Jesus Christ, who is all grace and truth, strength and courage and love,

Your fellow pilgrim,
Julian

28

Saying "Yes" to Love

A few weeks after I returned from sabbatical, Gideon returned to my companioning room. After we had spent some time catching up, I asked what he needed to attend to in the time we had remaining.

Gideon began by describing a struggle he had been facing at work. "I have been concerned for some time about the wages and conditions of the migrant workers, particularly the Chinese, who are brought to work on some of our buildings. But when I have expressed my concerns, our management has been adamant that the responsibility lies with the contractors." He fiddled with the sole of his shoe, then continued. "Our industrial relations director invited me to a meeting between the unions and the contractors, but I couldn't find the time to accompany her. It seemed a waste of time since all I could do was restate company policy." He ran his fingers through his hair and sighed. "Then the union representative approached me on-site because he'd heard about my concerns—but I was in a rush and said there was nothing I could do. I could tell he was upset, and I felt bad, but I brushed the matter aside by condemning the contractors."

Gideon looked up at me and said, "That was three strikes, you know!"

"Three strikes?" I responded.

"You know, then the cock crowed!" He hung his head, and as I watched over him, I felt shame resonating within my own heart.

"When, as you say, 'the cock crowed,' what did you notice happening within yourself?"

SAYING "YES" TO LOVE

Gideon shifted in his chair to gaze out the window. "You know, Julian, I have sat in this chair and spoken about all the big changes I see happening in my life, but betrayal comes in the things you choose not to notice."

Gideon lapsed into a ponderous silence. "I've come to see myself as a friend of people on the edge, but then I turn my back on a vulnerable and exploited group of visiting strangers to this land, people separated from their families and friends!" He looked up at me with tears in his eyes. "I have been too ashamed to tell you or my closest friends." He paused to wipe his eyes with a tissue. "But then I was reading the gospel account of Peter's betrayal of Jesus, and those 'three strikes' were brought right in front of my face. I felt like I was standing next to Peter and sharing in his shame."

"What happens as you look on that moment of 'three strikes' and share in Peter's shame?" I asked.

"The feeling of shame awakened me to what I had done—or failed to do—at work. And earlier, that would have sent me into a tailspin that could have lasted weeks, as if my ego were a balloon filled with my reputation, achievements, and the esteem of others—now popped by the pin of humiliation. But that humiliation tugged at my heart, and I saw that being 'deflated' wasn't the end of the story. I longed to stand with Peter in his reinstatement, when Jesus asked, 'Do you love me?'"[1] Gideon stopped, his lips moving silently, as he puzzled over this question. "'Do you love me more than your reputation in your firm?' Jesus is asking." Gideon looked at me, his eyes wide and wet with tears. "The questions that used to guide me were about how I felt about myself or how others felt about me, but again and again, I hear Jesus asking, 'Gideon, do you love me?' And my 'yes' is subdued and meek because it is coming from an ego that has been deflated."

I remained silent, holding prayerful space for Gideon to reflect on his words. After several minutes, he said, "When I said 'yes' to Jesus at work this past week, I didn't feel courageous, but meek. I decided to ask the union representative for an interpreter so that I could talk with the migrant workers, but the union rep was reluctant because he knew the workers were afraid. So I called a meeting with two of the contractors, and they threatened to report me to my superiors. As I stood in front of them, I felt powerless, so I prayed for a way to open, but instead of feeling stronger, I felt out of favor with Jesus. And so I prayed for his mercy. Then one of the contractor's mobile phone rang, and I stepped out of the office to give him some privacy. As I waited in the hallway praying for mercy, I felt that I had

1. John 21:16–17.

been reinstated, like the Apostle Peter." He took a deep breath and pressed his fingers against his eyes.

"You felt you had been reinstated, like the Apostle Peter," I reflected.

"When the door opened, I knew what I had to do. I invited the contractors to accompany me to my superior, stopping along the way to ask my secretary to call the industrial relations manager so she could join us. Then I told everyone who had gathered that no new contracts would be made on any of the building sites I managed if there were outstanding issues of pay or questionable conditions for migrant workers. I agreed to write to the union and apologize for my lack of action to date, and I also offered to establish personal contact with the migrant workers on my site. I knew my superior was upset, yet I felt neither afraid nor proud—just humbled by God's mercy." Gideon paused. "It was like my 'yes' to Jesus' question, 'Do you love me?'"

"Your 'yes' to Jesus' question, 'Do you love me?'" I reflected.

"When humiliation deflated my ego, it didn't destroy my identity, but humbled me and brought me back to the primary question of my identity and vocation in Jesus: 'Do you love me?'"

"Thanks be to God," I concluded.

"Yes, thanks be to God," Gideon agreed.

29

Do You Love Me?[1]

One of my guiding concerns is how I can engage with the kingdom life that comes my way—minute by hour by day—rather than reacting to pressing circumstances. I try to encourage this practice in pilgrims as well, so I was delighted to see Gideon responding to life in ways that were in tune with Jesus' prayer, "Your kingdom come. Your will be done, on earth as it is in heaven."[2]

Like Gideon, I had experienced humiliation in my life, and as I entered my evening time of prayer and reflection, I remembered my past tendency to react defensively to criticism, disregard, and humiliation. Gideon had stepped beyond such defensive reactions when he had compared his ego to a deflated balloon. As I attended to my own responses to shame and criticism, I saw a hot air balloon, with a little furnace to inflate it, quickly dropping from a great height as it rapidly deflated. As I held this picture in front of me, I wondered what fuel I could burn to reinflate my balloon. I knew that boosting my self-esteem with positive self-talk and external affirmations would not lift me to the heights of bold and courageous action.

Yet by sharing in the Apostle Peter's experience of betrayal, humiliation, and shame, Gideon had been invited beyond an ego-generated sense of himself to an awareness of Jesus' kingdom, where the internal dilemma that had deflated him was transformed into a positive external response that "refueled" him.

1. John 21:16.
2. Matt 6:10 NRSV.

PART V: PARTICIPATION

As I edged closer to Gideon's transformed response, I could see that I had witnessed an active, two-sided interchange of love between Gideon and Jesus. By attending to Jesus' question, "Do you love me?" Gideon had exchanged self-love and self-preservation for love of God and love of neighbor, in particular love for a marginalized group of workers whom he had failed. With the eyes of my heart opened, I could see that in this act Gideon was being empowered to embrace the greatest commandment: to love the Lord God with all his heart, soul, and strength, and to love his neighbor as himself.[3]

In the reciprocity of this embrace—Gideon's love for Jesus and Jesus' love for Gideon—the fullness of Gideon's lived experience, including his humiliation and his shame, had been gathered together and transformed into deeper life, an experience already enacted by Jesus through the reciprocal love he shared with his Father. This embrace of unity, spaciousness, and freedom was extended to Gideon, transforming all the daily experiences that might deflate, fragment, wound, or destabilize him into places of growth and "refueling." In the embrace of this love relationship, I could see that Gideon was becoming more and more like the Jesus he loved. What a mystery!

I marveled at the way the Spirit had moved through Gideon's faithful biblical reflection to guide him to the exact story he had needed at that particular moment in time: the gospel account of Peter's denial of Jesus, his shame and subsequent reinstatement. By bringing his lived experiences alongside Peter's, Gideon had stepped into the story, and the words had nourished his heart and consciousness.

Jesus' question to Peter had echoed through time and space to become Jesus' question to Gideon, and as I brought my lived experiences alongside Gideon's and Peter's during my evening prayer and reflection, I knew that the same question was being asked of me. I recalled how my fragile and bruised ego had often sought affirmation to reinflate me, cutting me off from a reciprocal relationship of love with Jesus. I didn't want to be guided by ego-generated stories about my failures and humiliations, which I knew would stifle my heart, cloud my consciousness, and make my posture defensive and hostile. As I reflected on Gideon's journey, I knew that I wanted to approach Jesus' question with the same meekness and humility. I longed that when criticisms and humiliations came, they would open me to my own poverty of spirit.

3. Matt 22:37–39.

In saying "yes" to Jesus, I knew that I was saying "yes" to a reciprocal relationship of love with the Trinity, which would expand my consciousness, stretch wide the "tent" of my heart, and guide me into a deeper experience of what is real. This "yes" would be the true source of my identity and would refuel my ongoing vocation.

30

Embracing Servanthood

At the beginning of our next session, Gideon seemed rather restless as he settled into the companioning chair. When I asked what he needed to attend to, he said, "I have been preoccupied with servanthood." He shifted in his chair.

"Preoccupied with servanthood," I echoed.

"I thought I had moved further on the road toward Jesus' servanthood," he said, bouncing his foot up and down, "because I love serving my team and fostering their creativity." He ran his fingers through his hair. "I know I've made some gains, but I have this niggling preoccupation that I'm not doing enough." He fidgeted in his chair.

"I wonder if you could invite the Spirit to guide you into this preoccupation," I suggested.

A space of silence followed, during which Gideon became more settled and relaxed. "Last Wednesday, Michael and Rob invited Sarah—a new friend from church—and me to a foot washing ceremony at their friends' community house."

"When I realized that Michael, Rob, and their friends with disabilities were going to wash our feet, I felt uncomfortable, but this discomfort disappeared as soon as Michael took my feet in his hands. Carefully and tenderly, he focused on washing my feet, as if he had all the time in the world. I was so moved that I started to weep, but then Jackie, who is wheelchair-bound and has no speech or control of her limbs, began to moan. Her assistant was quick to realize that she had not been given an opportunity to wash another's feet, and I was suddenly afraid that they would bring her to me. My fear made me feel so ashamed."

"Your fear made you feel ashamed," I reflected.

"Jackie did wash my feet, and it was—just as I feared—a slow and challenging task."

"As that event of Jackie washing your feet emerges before you, what draws your attention?"

I held the silence that followed in prayer, sensing that a significant shift was occurring within Gideon.

"I can only see Jackie. I know there are hands supporting her, but I cannot see them. She seems to want to catch my eye, and as my eyes meet hers..." His head dropped.

I waited, then asked, "As your eyes meet Jackie's, what draws your attention?"

"They are like deep pools that invite me to enter."

"And how do you respond to that invitation?" I asked, knowing that we had moved onto holy ground.

"I gaze within those eyes... and I see Jesus washing my feet."

"Jesus is washing your feet," I echoed.

"I feel the resistance and discomfort that Peter felt when Jesus washed his feet, so I say, 'You will never wash my feet.'"[1]

"Like Peter, you tell Jesus that he will never wash your feet."

"I feel my shame with Jackie resurfacing, so just like Peter, I ask Jesus to wash not only my feet but my hands and head as well.[2] As Jesus responds to my request, I feel the tenderness, care, and focus I felt with Michael. Now he is telling me to do for others what he has done for me."

"What do you notice now about your niggling preoccupation with servanthood?"

"I know that when Jesus washed his disciples' feet, he was stating where he had come from, where he was going, and what he had come to do. He was secure in his identity and purpose."

"As you notice that he was secure in his identity and purpose, what happens for you?" I asked.

"Rather than servanthood being a preoccupation"—he held up his right hand—"I desire purposefulness in my servanthood, which begins

1. John 13:8 NRSV.
2. John 13:9.

with letting him serve me." He held up his left hand, then studied his outstretched hands. "Jesus said, 'Whoever receives the person whom I send receives me,' and I see that he sent Jackie!"

31

Wash All of Me

As I entered my time of prayer and reflection that evening, I felt drawn to engage Jesus' incarnation and the fullness of his humanity through my senses. Moved by Gideon's account of his encounter with Michael, Jackie, and Jesus, I brought a bowl of water, soap, and a towel into my prayer space. When I had placed these elements on the coffee table beside me, I took off my shoes and socks.

In my opening prayer, I asked to come into the Lord's presence and behold His beauty. As I gazed at the bowl, soap, towel and my bare feet, I sensed that all of my physicality had a place in God's presence, but I also realized that this thought caused discomfort within me.

"Is there something here that I am blind to?" I wondered. Michael and Jackie had been servant messengers to Gideon, chosen from the margins of the world to proclaim the kingdom of God. Michael had offered Gideon tenderness and focused care. Jackie had offered Gideon her desire and intentionality. Though Gideon had felt discomfort with having his feet washed, Gideon's physicality had opened a doorway into his soul. As Gideon glimpsed Jesus through Jackie's eyes, his spirit was moved from a place of fear and shame to freedom and joy.

Through his brief encounter with Jesus, Gideon had realized that Jesus was washing his feet, and through this intimate exchange and divine touch, Gideon had found greater clarity and purposefulness for his active participation in the life of the kingdom. As a witness to the movement of grace in Gideon's life, I could pray with the Apostle Paul that the Holy God had made Gideon whole, uniting his body, soul, and spirit, equipping him for participation in the life of the kingdom, and preparing him for the return of Jesus Christ.[1]

I moved my gaze back to the bowl of water, soap, and towel that had drawn me into this reflection. As I sat looking at my bare feet, I heard an inner voice harping, "Your attention is wandering—get back to your prayer." "My feet are in the presence of God!" I replied, and that silenced the nagging. Feeling stirred to stand, I told my inner critic, "I can continue my prayer even while walking!" As I walked out of my office onto the lawn, I thanked God for the warm night and refreshing breeze and for the feeling of grass and soil on my bare feet. "God is present," I reminded myself. "I am in God's temple—all of me!"

As I continued to walk and breathe deeply, the tension I had been holding in my body dissipated. As I breathed in the presence of God and exhaled praise, the peace of the Spirit fell upon me in the warmth of the early evening and the sprinkling rain that fell from the sky. As I returned to my office, with grass and soil clinging to my feet, my eyes once again fell upon the bowl, soap, and towel. As I washed and dried my feet, I remembered Paul's prayer of "wholeness" and "holiness" and Peter's desire to be wholly washed by Jesus. I prayed that the whole of my person might be redeemed, restored, and reconciled, so that my whole self could become holy. As I tipped the bowl of dirty water onto the garden and hung the towel to dry, I reflected on how these everyday elements had been used in the service of holiness. God had extended my experience of the incarnation, inviting me to embody wholeness—and holiness—in my physical self. A passage from Isaiah provided the benediction for my prayer and reflection: "How beautiful upon the mountains are the feet of the messenger who announces peace, who brings good news, who announces salvation, who says to Zion, 'Your God reigns.'"[2] May my feet join with those of the messenger, and may God reign over the whole of me! Amen.

---

1. 1 Thess 5:23 MSG (adapted).
2. Isa 52:7 NRSV.

32

Can You Drink from This Cup?[1]

Four weeks later, at the beginning of our session, Gideon said, "This Easter, I've been struggling to stay engaged with Jesus' story." He sighed, then fell silent.

As I watched over Gideon through this long period of weighty silence, I was aware that being invited to guide this young man through his awakening to his life and to faith was a sacred privilege.

"Sarah," Gideon began at last, "decided to journey with Mary Magdalene through Jesus' passion and resurrection. At first, I felt sidelined by her intention to make this her focus." He paused. "But I realized that it was an opportunity for me to journey with Jesus. I felt rather sleepy at the Maundy Thursday vigil, and early in the evening I nodded off, with my head on Sarah's shoulder. When I woke with a start, I remembered Jesus' words to his disciples: 'So, could you not stay awake with me one hour? Stay awake and pray that you may not come into the time of trial; the spirit indeed is willing, but the flesh is weak.'[2] But it was such a challenge to watch and pray, with my mind flitting into petty and self-absorbed pursuits. I was so frustrated!"

I could feel the resonance of this contradiction within myself. "Could you say something about that frustration?"

"It is the frustration I feel when my attention is drawn from an important task to something I consider trivial and unproductive," Gideon replied.

---

1. Matt 20:22.
2. Matt 26:40–41.

"What happens as you reenter the frustration you felt as you tried to watch and pray?" I asked.

"It seems like such a contradiction," he said. "But as I bring my attention to Jesus, I see a very small boy crawling through the legs of adults to see what they are looking at. When he reaches the front of the crowd, he pops his head out and says, 'Look, I'm here.' Then the boy grows bigger, and I am with the disciples, watching over Jesus, though they are all asleep."

"As you see the boy push his way through the crowd and watch him grow bigger, and then realize that you are with the disciples watching over Jesus, what do you notice about yourself?" I asked.

"Thursday night, I got cross with my distractions and pushed them away—that's where the frustration was. Now I see that my distractions were the boy, and rather than dismissing him crossly, I need to give him space to grow up so he can encounter the mystery of what is before him." Gideon took a deep breath. "Now I can celebrate the richness of Thursday night. My growing up began with a crisis and a search for something deep within myself with which I had not kept faith. This was followed by a period of suffering and turmoil. At the service, I wondered how I would ever be able to drink from life's cup the way Jesus had."

Gideon looked toward me, his eyes wide. "I think Jesus is asking me if I can drink from his cup."

"What do you choose to do?" I asked, leaning back in my chair to wait prayerfully for his response.

Gideon entered his inner world so deeply that it took him several minutes to answer. "He is not asking me to exchange one cup for another. He is showing me that my little cup of suffering is already within his, and my drinking from his cup begins with the anguish I already know." Gideon paused. "I choose to drink from my Master's cup," he said solemnly.

I felt deeply resonant as I imagined Gideon drinking from Jesus' cup.

"Now I am ready for my Gethsemane work," Gideon said after a long silence.

My heart beat faster as I echoed, "You are ready for your Gethsemane work."

"I am ready to step into my master's struggle—that is, the part of his struggle I need to own for myself."

I prayed for mercy and asked Jesus to help me cooperate with this movement of grace and stay with Gideon's story thread. Taking that brief moment to bring my complete focus to the pilgrim in front of me, I asked, "As you step into your master's struggle, what draws your attention?"

Gideon closed his eyes. "It's a life-and-death struggle."

"As you remain with that life-and-death struggle, what happens to you?"

"I'm gazing into a swirling vortex." He dropped his head as he often did when entering his active imagination.

I sought to hold a safe external space for Gideon as he journeyed into this swirling vortex, aware that he was held by hands far greater than my own. "As you gaze into that swirling vortex, what do you notice?" I asked.

"It is my dark cavern with its frozen lake swirling around, but it smells like death, and there is a magnet drawing everything dark and evil down into its center."

"As you see that darkness and evil being drawn down into the vortex, what happens to you?" I asked.

"The swirling has slowed down, and I can see my own inner darkness and addictiveness over the past several years swirling around before me. I desperately want to run away from all this."

"As you reencounter your own darkness in that swirl and acknowledge that you want to run away from it, what do you notice yourself doing?" I asked.

"I turn away, but something is inviting me to look at it again."

Sensing Gideon's distress, I prayed silently until he spoke again. "As I look again, I am falling over an edge into the darkness, but I feel like I am falling into something greater."

I marveled at Gideon's insightfulness as I waited for him to continue.

"Everything in me keeps saying, 'turn and run away.'"

"You turned before, but you did not run away," I observed, "because something invited you to look again."

"It is Jesus," responded Gideon. "He is preparing to leap into that huge vortex, and he is telling all of us to get going, because his betrayer is at hand. I don't want to be his betrayer!" he cried out. "I want to go with my master!"

After another long silence, during which I reflected on Gideon's presence before me and imagined him being held beneath the shelter of his master's wings, Gideon said, "Amen," bringing our session to a close.

33

Turning toward Jerusalem

By the time I came home to my reflection and prayer that evening, I was eager to reflect on Gideon's Easter journey. As I gave thanks for the divine guidance Gideon had received, I was drawn to Gideon's metaphor of Jesus leaping into the vortex and Gideon's sensation that as he fell, he was falling into something greater.

As I brought my attention to this metaphor, I saw an image of Gideon as a mountaineer clamoring up treacherous slopes. As he rested before the last stretch of his ascent, gazing at the distant mountain still shrouded in mist, I saw someone stooping over him to massage his bruised and sore feet. As he scrambled up the final steep slopes, I could see footholds carved into the rock by the guide who was climbing ahead of him. As dark storm clouds gathered overhead and thunder echoed off the exposed rock, I saw bolts of lightning and, in their crackling light, a slender golden thread snaking along the winding path, leading him forward one step at a time.

At the summit, Gideon rested against a rock as he waited for dawn to fold back the darkness. When dawn finally washed the sky in golden light, a gentle breeze brushed away the veil of thin clouds, and Gideon saw peaks he had never seen before towering above the one he had just climbed. He shielded his eyes from the glare of the sun's early morning fire, and his spirit quickened with a desire to climb the massive peak before him, now clad in gold. Before the breath of dawn veiled the distant mountain in mist, he saw a slender thread of gold stretching from his perch on the rocks, down through the valley, and back up the mountain's summit.

Rousing myself from active imagining, I remembered that Gideon had not seen himself climbing "Easter Mountain" during our morning session—it had been my imagery! Instead, Gideon had encountered a dark and swirling vortex and had sought to stay close to Jesus through his Gethsemane struggle, responding to the question, "Are you able to drink the cup that I am about to drink?"[1] This morning, Gideon could have turned away from that question—and from Jesus as he asked the question. As I remained close to Gideon in that crucial moment in Gethsemane, I saw in myself the desire to turn back and walk away from the darkness and death smells. I saw this desire to turn back in the disciples as they balked at Jesus' talk of turning towards Jerusalem, suffering at the hand of the religious and political rulers, and being put to death as an ordinary criminal. How few are willing to gather around the soon-to-be crucified Lord! Jesus does not ask his ardent young disciples, "Can you carry my banner?" or "Will you raise my banner on the battlefield?" Instead, he asks, "Can you drink from my cup? Can you choose suffering over power?"

Like the disciples, Gideon's first impulse was to walk away, but then he chooses to drink from Christ's cup, and in the suffering of Christ he glimpses his own suffering. Though he is invited to follow an unknown path, he trusts that his Master Guide will lead him safely home. This is my path, too, and like Gideon, I choose to follow my guide and to drink from his cup of redemptive suffering.

---

1. Matt 20:22 NRSV.

Epilogue
Making Way for the New

Many years later, after I suffered a stroke, Gideon visited me faithfully in the hospital. I had stopped meeting with him as a guide and spiritual director years earlier, but we had remained good friends through my retirement. His presence filled the sterile walls of my hospital room with life, and though I could no longer speak well, I could still think—and Gideon talked with me as if he could hear my thoughts without my having to speak them.

Though in my frailty I sometimes envied the strength of Gideon's active limbs, I found deep peace in his presence. Unable to verbally express the stirrings of my inner world, I wept often, and my medical attendants would pause and with compassion dry my eyes, assuming that I was grieving. But Gideon seemed to understand that my interior ground was being prepared for the planting of something new. He had not forgotten the weeping of the woman of the lake, and he knew that joy and pain, suffering and gratitude, and life and death are intertwined.

News of Gideon's daily life with Sarah and their six- and eight-year-old children brought me great joy, particularly when he spoke of the special relationship that had developed between his mother and her grandchildren. Where there had once been distance and smothering with Gideon, there was now affection and spaciousness. Gideon's father had passed after a long illness—before his grandchildren were born, but not before the Spirit had melted the alienation that had kept him distant from Gideon for so long.

During tonight's visit, Gideon held my hand in the deepening silence of the evening as I wept—with gratitude and sorrow—over the flood of memories filling my mind. Gideon made no effort to hide his tears, and in the silence, we shared a long communion as he paused from his active family life and I readied my aching body to leave this world, with neither fear nor regret. In our hands was the begging bowl of communion and love that had brought meekness to our lives and humility to our friendship. I knew this man would miss me, and the knowledge of his love for me would carry me peacefully to the end of my earthly journey.

When it was time for Gideon to leave, he reached in his pocket and produced a bottle of oil, then spread oil across the palms of my hands and traced the sign of the cross on my forehead. Rising, he held my hands between his own and prayed the Lord's Prayer, then kissed my forehead where he had marked it with the cross. I squeezed his hand, and he said, "God speed you, my friend."

I followed his figure down the corridor, where he turned and stood, looking back, then waved and continued on his way. In his face I had seen the radiance of his master, and a deep, warm peace washed over me. I knew that I would most likely not see Gideon again in this world, yet I knew that he had been loved into existence by his Creator-God, and I, too, could rest in that love all the way through to my last living breath.

As I settled back into my pillows, the peace and contentment remained. Though it would not always be easy for Gideon, he had been chosen by the Creator of all life—and he had chosen to keep journeying toward the deeper life that had desired him into existence. We both had been guides in helping each other find our way home. As sleep overcame me, I repeated the final words of Gideon's parting prayer: "For thine is the kingdom, the power and the glory, forever and ever. Amen."

Bibliography

Blake, William. *The Poems of William Blake*. Edited by John Sampson. London: Chatto and Windus, at the Florence Press, 1921.
Brown, Christopher. *Reflected Love: Companioning in the Way of Jesus*. Eugene, OR: Wipf & Stock, 2012.
John of the Cross. "The Living Flame of Love." In *Centred on Love: The Poems of St John of the Cross*, translated by Marjorie Flower, 22. Varroville, NSW: Carmelite Nuns, 2002.
———. *Selected Writings*. Translated by Kieran Kavanaugh. New York: Paulist, 1987.
Lewis, C. S. *Surprised by Joy: The Shape of My Early Life*. London: G. Bles, 1955.
Watts, Isaac. "When I Survey the Wondrous Cross." In *Hymns and Spiritual Songs*. London: printed by J. Humfreys, for John Lawrence, at the Angel in the Poultrey, 1707.

www.ingramcontent.com/pod-product-compliance
Lightning Source LLC
Chambersburg PA
CBHW030859170426
43193CB00009BA/676